LICENSE PLATE BOOK

BY

THOMSON C. MURRAY
Edited by/ Michael C. Wiener
Designed by/ William L.Cummings
Graphics by/ Frank DiGiovanni

Interstate Directory Publishing Company,Inc.
420 Jericho Turnpike
Jericho, New York 11753
516-822-5966, fax 5962

The author wishes to thank The American Association of Motor Vehicle Administrators for their help both with this and previous editions. The Motor Vehicle departments of all 51 U.S and 12 Canadian jurisdictions have been wonderful this year as in the past, and Tom Kneitel (K2AES) who provided the radio material and shared his insight into the world of AM. A word of appreciation is due to to Chuck Sakryd, Dave Lincoln, Mike Apgar, Keith Marvin, Mike Natale, Bob Bittner, Dave Fraser, Darrell Dady, Kit Sage, Roy Carson, and Richard Draper who are just a few of the many ALPCA members who have helped and encouraged me in this project. Special thanks to the Turtle Mountain Tribal Council for permission to include their plate.

Tom and Judy Kneitel , Frank and Lori at Adcraft , Laura Kucklinca, Michael Wiener and Bill Cummings are all part of the team that makes this book possible.

Dedicated to
Mary Thompson Murray
lovingly remembered as

Geggie

The license plates illustrated in this book are a representative sample selected by the author. They illustrate a typical type of plate issued by a jurisdiction. If the alpha and/or numeric characters duplicate a particular plate currently in use it is strictly coincidental. The material in this book was compiled from information provided by State, Provincial Territorial and Federal motor Vehicle authorities. Interstate Directory Publishing Company Inc. is not responsible for any inadvertent inaccuracies or omission.

ISBN 0-962-99-621-1

1992 Edition

Trade paper edition ISBN 0-87131-710-9 is distributed to the book trade by:

M. Evans and Company
216 East 49th Street
New York, New York 10017

Manufactured in the United States of America

9 8 7 6 5 4 3 2

INTRODUCTION

License plates have hidden meanings that can be recognized by law enforcement, serious collectors and motor vehicle authorities. This book explains how states and provinces code their plates so you, like the authorities, will be able to look at a plate and tell such things as:

- In what county a vehicle is registered.
- Occupation of the owner.
- Special plates and what they mean.   **719766**
- Age, weight and vehicle use restrictions.
- How to recognize a rented car.
- State, City, Federal Government, Diplomatic codes.
- Indian tribes.
- First initial of the owners last name or birth month.

Also:
How to trace the name and address of an owner by the plate number.
How to get personalized plates and what they cost.

How to "read" a license plate

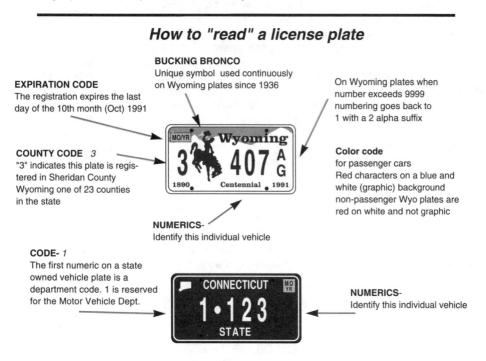

BUCKING BRONCO
Unique symbol used continuously on Wyoming plates since 1936

On Wyoming plates when number exceeds 9999 numbering goes back to 1 with a 2 alpha suffix

EXPIRATION CODE
The registration expires the last day of the 10th month (Oct) 1991

COUNTY CODE *3*
"3" indicates this plate is registered in Sheridan County Wyoming one of 23 counties in the state

Color code
for passenger cars
Red characters on a blue and white (graphic) background non-passenger Wyo plates are red on white and not graphic

NUMERICS-
Identify this individual vehicle

CODE- *1*
The first numeric on a state owned vehicle plate is a department code. 1 is reserved for the Motor Vehicle Dept.

NUMERICS-
Identify this individual vehicle

---

1. Look at the color combinations. Each section explains how jurisdictions use color combinations to distinguish classes of vehicle.

2. If you see a caption (a word embossed on a plate) you do not understand, look under the Distinctive Caption section and it will be explained. For example BAILEE in Rhode Island is a caption for a repossessor plate.

3. Codes- Look at the combination of alpha and numeric characters (letters and numbers) and check the code section to see if there are any hidden meanings

LICENSE PLATES AND HOW TO READ THEM

The popular name for the metal plate affixed to a vehicle is a "license plate". In many states, particularly in the South, these are commonly referred to as "license tags". Actually the vehicle is not licensed, the driver is. Every vehicle is "registered" with authorities, and the metal plate is issued to identify the each particular vehicle and indicate that it has met certain conditions and the owner has paid required registration fees and taxes. The driver is "licensed" and the metal plate is a "registration plate", but for almost ninety years the public has used the term "license plate" and we won't try to correct things now.

License plates are issued to indicate proper registration of a vehicle, they also often contain codes which can tell you a lot about the vehicle and the owner. In fact there is an incredible "hidden language" of license plates which this book has been designed to explain.

Although every state and provincial motor vehicle administration uses a different system to issue plates and assign numbers, they all recognize the need for law enforcement authorities to distinguish classes of vehicles by simply glancing at the plate. There are three methods to make these distinctions:

COLOR- Different combinations are used for classes of vehicles.

CAPTIONS- Words are embossed to give special information

CODES- Series of letters and numbers (alpha, numeric characters) used in the plate numbering system that are reserved for special identification.

The material in this book has been gathered from Motor Vehicle administrations of all 50 states, District of Columbia, 12 Canadian provinces and territories as well as contributions of members of Automobile License Plate Collectors Association (ALPCA). It is organized to explain how every jurisdiction (state or province) uses these three techniques to help authorities "read" a license plate and instantly tell if it is a valid registration, what county it comes from, weight class, use restrictions, occupation and any other special information that may be available about the owner and his vehicle.

PASSENGER CARS

All U.S. and Canadian jurisdictions currently issue permanent or semi-permanent license plates that are used for a number of years and revalidated annually or bi-annually with decals. Of the 51 U.S. jurisdictions 31 issue two plates, while the remaining 20 require on only one plate per vehicle. The trend in recent years has been away from two plates primarily due to the increasing cost of plate manufacture. The things to look for on passenger plates are:

COUNTY CODES
OCCUPATION CODES
EXPIRATION CODES
GOVERNMENT DEPARTMENT CODES
CODES RESERVED FOR SPECIAL GROUPS AND OFFICIALS

In many states you can tell in which county a vehicle is registered, if the owner is a member of a special group or organization, and the age and weight of the vehicle. All this information and much more is available from just looking at a license plate and referring to this book.

TRUCKS TRAILERS AND OTHER HEAVY VEHICLES

Trucks, truck tractors, buses, trailers and other heavy vehicles, unlike private passenger cars, must pay a variety of taxes based on weight, miles driven and fuel consumption in addition to registration fees.This is why commercial license plates are often a different color and changed more frequently than passenger plates.

Every state has at least two sources of revenue that is collected from commercial vehicles: registration fees and fuel consumption taxes. A few states have a third level of taxation based on a formula of miles run and tons carried.

In addition to a registration license plate, a commercial vehicle operating only within the state where it is registered must display a decal or plate showing registration for the payment of fuel and any other taxes or inspection required by the particular state. This is usually done by a small plate issued by the Public Service Commission (PSC) or Tax Commissioner or a decal on the cab or bumper of the vehicle.

VEHICLES OPERATING INTERSTATE

Private passenger cars can cross state lines and drive freely anywhere within the United States because every state has agreed to honor the registration of a car registered in every other state. This is called full reciprocity.

Commercial vehicles do not enjoy this same freedom of movement over state lines. States rely heavily on commercial vehicle registration and tax revenue to defray the cost of highway construction and maintenance. They insist that all trucks and other heavy vehicles using their highways pay their fair share. As a result, a commercial or heavy vehicle cannot operate in another state unless there is some agreement between the two states providing for reciprocity (sharing) of registration fees. This sharing of registration and tax revenue is called apportionment or prorating.

Currently most states have some sort of agreement with every other state to grant full reciprocity or share registration fees and tax revenue based on actual highway use. This is a complicated problem and difficult for both state authorities and the trucking industry to administer and enforce. This situation is one reason you often can see multiple plates and decals on vehicles operating interstate .

In recent years 42 states and Alberta have joined the International Registration Plan (IRP) where only one license plate captioned APPORTIONED is issued by the state where the vehicle is based. This is the only plate that has to be displayed by heavy vehicles operating interstate within the member states.

GREEN ON WHITE

APPORTIONED

PLATES AND PARKING FOR THE DISABLED

The automobile gives a disabled person in the United States the chance to enjoy independence and mobility. They are given special parking privileges, and every effort is made to meet their needs and still not inconvenience the general public.

The familiar wheelchair symbol is used worldwide. The official name of the symbol is International Symbol of Access (ISA) and appears on signs, placards and license plates to identify vehicles transporting disabled persons and the parking areas reserved for their use.

Until 1991 there were no uniform guidelines covering the administration of special parking for the disabled. Every state handled the situation in their individual manner. Some of the problems are abuse of special parking by unauthorized people using disabled plates and special parking plates designed and issued in one state were often not recognized or honored in other states. The Department of Transportation (DOT) developed a uniform system for disabled parking which became federal law March 11, 1991. Under this law every qualified applicant for special parking privileges will have the choice of either a special plate embossed with the ISA or a parking placard to hang from the rearview mirror on the inside of the vehicle. The advantage of the placard is it can be moved to any vehicle, and the car remains unmarked when the placard is not displayed. The law also permits two placards to be issued to one individual if needed.

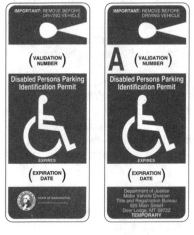

Blue placards are issued only for permanent disability and are renewed periodically by the issuing jurisdiction.

Red placards are issued for temporary disabilities and are valid for a maximum period of six months.

These representative samples of disabled persons parking permits from two jurisdictions (Washington and Montana) were provided through the courtesy of:

The American Association of Motor Vehicle Administrators, Arlington VA

Actual size of placard is 3 1/2 x 9 1/4 in.

Manufacturing and Reflectorization

It is still true that most license plates are manufactured in correctional institutions, however there are some private contractors who also make plates for the states. License plates are made by stamping letters and numbers (characters) into a metal blank and painting. After stamping the whole plate is painted and a contrasting color is added to the raised characters by roller.

In the 1940's two New England states added a reflective coating to their plates to make them easier to see at night. The reflective coating is made of millions of tiny glass beads that refract (bend) the light which reflects back many times brighter than from a plain painted surface.

Plates that are painted and have the reflective glass beads added to just the raised characters are partially-reflective. New materials have been developed that can be printed many colors and stamped and still retain the reflective quality of the glass beads. This special sheeting is pre-printed and then adhered to the metal blank and stamped. The raised characters are colored with ink and the whole plate is coated with a clear protective material. This type of plate is referred to as fully-reflectorized.

Reflectorization is an important safety factor and of significant value to law enforcement. Just consider a police officer checking isolated parking lots at night. With reflectorized plates identification can quickly and easily be achieved with headlights or spotlight from the patrol car. Fully reflectorized plates can be seen at long distance at night, and can be very colorful. The only drawback is special reflective sheeting adds to the expense of manufacturing plates.

DIPLOMATIC LICENSE PLATES

In 1985 the United States Department of State began issuing distinctive red white and blue license plates to vehicles owned by a foreign mission.These diplomatic tags have an oversize letter code (A, C, D, S) which appears as a prefix on foreign mission plates nationwide, and a suffix issued to the United Nations.The code is: A-Assembly,C-Consul, D-Diplomat, S- Mission staff.The two letters used in the plate numbering system is a country code. The State Department can change combinations whenever needed, however here is a recent list.

FORIEGN CONSUL

DIPLOMAT

NON-DIPLOMATIC STAFF

UNITED NATIONS
SECRETARIAT

UNITED NATIONS DIPLOMAT

FORIEGN MISSION TO U.N.
& FAMILY MEMBERS

AA CONGO	**FN** MALTA	**KW** SEYCHELLES	**QX** PAKISTAN
AC IVORY COAST	**FP** MOROCCO	**KX** S. YEMEN	**QY** S. YEMEN
AF JAPAN	**FR** PHILIPPINES	**LC** VENEZUELA	**QZ** INDONESIA
AH MADAGASCAR	**FS** NETHERLANDS	**LG** TURKEY	**RB** RWANDA
AJ PANAMA	**FT** QATAR	**LD** VIET NAM	**RC** ST VINCENT
AK CAPE VERDE	**FV** SRI LANKA	**LH** ISRAEL	**RD** SENEGAL
AQ SYRIA	**FW** HOLY SEE (VATICAN)	**LJ** ISRAEL	**RL** URUGUAY
AU UGANDA	**FX** SIERRA LEONE	**LK** DEL. TO EEC	**SG** ISRAEL
AV ISRAEL	**FY** SOUTH AFRICA	**LW** GERMANY	**ST** DOMINICIA
AW ORG. OF AFRICAN UNITY	**FZ** SURINAME	**MK** DJIBOUTI	**SX** USSR
BL SOUTH AFRICA	**GC** SWEDEN	**ML** DIEGO GARCIA	**TG** MALI
BY SOLOMON ISLANDS	**GD** UKRAINE	**MN** UNITED NATIONS	**TF** ALGERIA
BZ IRAQ	**GG** ZAMBIA	**MP** BAHAMAS	**TG** CANADA
CB CAMBODIA (KAMPUCHEA)	**GM** TURKEY	**MQ** MONACO	**TH** EGYPT
CC ETHIOPIA	**GP** ALBANIA	**MW** MALDIVES	**TJ** GERMANY
CS AFGHANISTAN	**GQ** NORTH KOREA	**NA** OMAN	**TK** NETH. ANTIL.
CT BHUTAN	**HL** ST. LUCIA	**NB** NEW GUINEA	**TL** EL SALVADOR
CU BOTSWANA	**HN** MONGOLIA	**NC** PARAGUAY	**TM** ICELAND
CV BURMA	**HV** BELGIUM	**ND** ROMANIA	**TN** NEPAL
CW CAMEROON	**HW** GUATEMALA	**NQ** ANGOLA	**TP** MAURITANIA
CX BURUNDI	**HX** BENIN	**PA** AUSTRIA	**TR** ITALY
CY CHINA	**HY** GUINEA BISSAU	**PB** BARBADOS	**TS** IRAQ
DA COLOMBIA	**HZ** HAITI	**PC** BELIZE	**TT** GUYANA
DB COSTA RICA	**JB** HONDURAS	**PD** BERMUDA	**TU** GUINEA
DC CUBA	**JC** KUWAIT	**PF** BOLIVIA	**TV** GHANA
DD CYPRUS	**JD** MAURITIUS	**PG** BYELORUSSIA	**TW** GAMBIA
DF DOM. REP	**JF** NIGERIA	**PH** CZECH.	**TX** FINLAND
DG EQUADOR	**JG** PORTUGAL	**PI** ISRAEL	**TY** GRENADA
DH FR. CARRIBEAN	**JH** SOMALIA	**PK** NORWAY	**TZ** PERU
DI ISRAEL.	**JJ** CHAD	**PL** CHILE	**UA** BAHRAIN
DJ FRANCE	**JK** TURKEY	**PM** BRUNEI	**UF** ESTONIA
DK GREECE	**JM** YUGOSLAVIA	**PR** ARGENTINA	**UH** SPAIN
DL INDIA	**JP** TUNISIA	**PS** ZIMBABWE	**UX** TRINIDAD & TOBAGO
DM IRAN	**JQ** TOGO	**PV** ZAIRE	**VF** THAILAND
DN DENMARK	**KQ** EQU.GUINEA	**QA** N. YEMEN	**VG** TANZANIA
DP BANGLADESH	**KH** HUNGARY	**QD** BURKINA FASO	**VH** SWITZERLAND
FC FORMER USSR	**KJ** LITHUANIA	**QL** ST. CHRIS	**VJ** BRAZIL
FF ANTIGUA	**KK** FIJI	**QM** BULGARIA	**VK** SINGAPORE
FG CEN.AF.REP.	**KL** JORDAN	**QN** LAOS	**VL** SWAZILAND
FH IRELAND	**KM** JAMAICIA	**QP** LESOTHO	**WB** U.A.R.
FI ISRAEL	**KN** GABON	**QQ** LESOTHO	**WD** S KOREA
FJ LEBANON	**KP** LUXEMBOURG	**QR** MALAWI	**WM** W. SAMOA
FK KENYA	**KR** MALAYSIA	**QS** MOZAMBIQUE	**WZ** UNIT. KNGDM
FL LIBERIA	**KS** MEXICO	**QT** NEW ZEALAND	**XF** TURKEY
FM LIBYA	**KT** NAMIBIA	**QU** NICARAGUA	**XZ** AUSTRALIA
	KU SAO TOME / PRINCIPE	**QV** NIGER	**YM** HONG KONG
	KV SAUDI ARABIA	**QW** POLAND	

UNITED STATES GOVERNMENT VEHICLES

The General Services Administration (GSA) maintains vehicles in motor pools across the country for official use of Government agencies and departments.

All plates are blue on white. The prefix indicates vehicle type.

G11 - Sedans; intermediate; subcompact
G12 - Sedans; compact
G14 - Sedans; standard (regular)
G21 - Station wagons; subcompact/compact
G23 - Station wagons; standard regular
G31 - Ambulances; buses
G41 - Trucks- cargo 1/2 ton and under (4x2)
G42 - Trucks- cargo 3/4 ton (4x2)
G43 - Trucks- cargo 1 ton (4x2)

G61 - Trucks - cargo 1/2 ton and under (4x4)
G62 - Trucks - cargo 3/4 ton (4x4)
G63 - Trucks - cargo 1 ton (4x4)
G71 - Trucks - cargo 12,500 - 23,999 GVW
G81 - Trucks - cargo 24,000+ GVW gasoline
G82 - Trucks - Cargo 24,000+ GVW diesel
G91 - Trucks, trailers , semi-trailers (special purpose type vehicles)

Federal Government owned vehicles owned by individual departments can be identified by the alpha prefix code as follows:

A - Agriculture
ACT - Action
AF - Air Force
C - Commerce
CA - Civil Aeronautics Board
CE - Corps of Engineers
CPSC - Consumer Product Safety Comm.
CS - Civil Service Commission
D - Defense
DA - Defense Contract Audit Agency
DOT - Dept. of Transportation
DA - Defense Supply Agency
E - Energy Research & Development Admin.
EO - Executive office of the President
    Council of Economic Advisors
    National Security Council
    Office of Management & Budget
EPA - Environmental Protection Agency
EPS - Executive protection Services
FA - Federal Aviation Administration
FC - Federal Communications Commission
FD - Federal Deposit Insurance Corp.
FM - Federal Mediation &Conciliation Serv.
FP - Federal Power Commission
FR - Federal Reserve System
FT - Federal Trade Commission
G - Interagency Motor Pool System
GA - General Accounting Office
GP - Government Printing Office
GS - General Services Administration
H - Housing & Urban Development

HW - Health, Education & Welfare
I - Interior
IA - Information Agency
IC - Interstate Commerce Commission
J - Justice
JB - Judicial Branch
L - Labor
LA - D of C Redevelopment Land Agency
LB - Legislative Branch
N - Navy
NA - Nat'l. Aeronautics & Space Admin.
NG - National Guard Bureau
NH - Nat'l Cap. Housing Authority
NL - National Labor Relations Board
NP - Nat'l Cap. Planning Comm.
NRC - Nuclear Regulatory Comm.
NS - National Science Commission
OEO - Office Economic Opportunity
P - Postal Service
PC -Panama Canal Company
RB - Renegotiation Board
RR - Railroad Retirement Board
S - State Department
SB - Small Business Administration
SE - Securities & Exchange Commission
SH - Soldiers & Airmen's' Home
SI - Smithsonian Institution Ntl Gallery Art.
T - Treasury
TV - Tennessee Valley Authority
VA - Veterans Administration
W - Army

Adding To Your Trip With Radio

You probably know the advantages of a CB or cellular radio in your vehicle. CB Channel 9 is where you call for help if you have a problem (many police agencies and emergency teams monitor this channel), or you can dial up 911 on your cellular. CB channel 19 is where the truckers and cars chat and announce advisories about road conditions. But did you know that your car's AM broadcast radio can also add to your trip?

North America is a wonderful conglomeration of local dialects, regional identities, and hometown folks. If you go zipping through an area at 55 MPH on the Interstate while listening to taped or CD music, you're definitely missing a lot. You're seeing the panoramic views through your windows, but the sound track is all wrong! You're missing out on the sounds that should accompany and enhance these sights.

Shut off that tape deck or CD player. Turn on the vehicle's AM radio and delight in hearing the magnificent sounds that portray the flavor of the area in which you are driving. You'll share in the music, the hometown news, the views of national and international events, the local sports scores, hear about products and services you never knew existed. And you'll hear everything described in one of the many unique and colorful regional accents that are to be enjoyed throughout the United States and Canada. You'll learn something about the people and places you are seeing if you listen to their music, opinions and voices.

You can even find out about shops, restaurants, events, or other attractions that you'll want to visit; places that aren't listed in tourist guides!

In this edition of The License Plate Book we have included the call letters, locations and frequencies of some of the most powerful stations in each state and province that should be the easiest for you to hear when you drive. There are, of course, many other stations to hear. You can tune across the band to see how many you can discover. No matter what you tune in, be assured that you will find it thoroughly enjoyable, and also vastly different from any broadcast station you're used to hearing, regardless of where you come from. In fact, quite different than when you tune in a station from 500 miles further down the Interstate.

When you drive at night, you'll have a totally different experience than when you listen to your AM radio during daytime. At night, the most powerful broadcasters can be heard over distances considerably further than their normal coverage during daylight hours. This is because at night smaller local stations sharing their frequencies either reduce their power or leave the air. Also, the powerful signals are helped along by certain signal-reflecting areas of the ionosphere, high above the earth, that activate at night. During nighttime hours, "powerhouse" and "clear channel" stations may be heard for hundreds or even thousands of miles. The stations listed in this edition include those stations most likely to be heard at night over such wide areas.

Truckers, especially, like to listen to the powerhouse stations at night while they traverse the Interstates."The Road Gang" program is heard coast-to-coast from a network of just four stations WWVA (1130) Wheeling WV, KRVN (880) Lexington NE, WWL (870) New Orleans LA , KTNN (660) Window Rock AZ. You can listen to country music and road conditions from Maine to Arizona.

Day or night, your vehicle's AM radio is only an arm's length away from the drivers seat. Reach over and turn it on. It adds a great new dimension to enjoying, and getting the most from, your excursion down the highways of North America.

ALABAMA

STATE ROUTE MARKER

HUNTSVILLE
BIRMINGHAM

21

WAPI 1070 Birmingham
WVOK 690 Birmingham
WYDG 850 Birmingham
WAAJ 1550 Huntsville

AM RADIO

ALABAMA
Heart of Dixie
MO · 25AAA01 · YR

1 PLATE VALIDATED
BY 2 DECALS
NEW ISSUE 1992

HEART OF DIXIE
43AA 843
MO · **Alabama** · YR

PASSENGER REGULAR

HEART OF DIXIE
DIXIE
MO · **Alabama** · YR

PERSONALIZED

HEART OF DIXIE · **Alabama** ·
&. 18100
MO HANDICAPPED YR

HANDICAPPED

HEART OF DIXIE · **Alabama** ·
DISABLED VETERAN
5200W
MO · · YR

DISABLED VETERAN

HEART OF DIXIE · **Alabama** ·
17700 MU
· MUNICIPAL ·

CITY OWNED PERMANENT

HEART OF DIXIE · **Alabama** ·
S 20400
· ·

STATE OWNED PERMANENT

HEART OF DIXIE · **Alabama** ·
D 50001
NOV · DEALER · 92

DEALER
ANNUAL PLATE

NOV · **Alabama** · 92
Heart of Dixie
80X9 100

TRUCKS, TRUCK-TRACTORS
X1-X9 ANNUAL PLATE

NOV · **Alabama** · 92
Heart of Dixie
80XL 100
· RESTRICTED ·

TRACTOR (ANNUAL)
RESTRICTED TO WITHIN
15 MILES OF CITY LIMITS

NOV · **Alabama** · 92
Heart of Dixie
80L2 100
· FOREST ·

FOREST PRODUCTS
TRUCK L1-L2
ANNUAL PLATE

NOV · **Alabama** · 92
Heart of Dixie
X8 66173
· APPORTIONED ·

TRUCKS, TRUCK-TRACTORS
INTERSTATE X-XA, X1-X9

OCT · **ALABAMA** · 92
S25
· NATIONAL GUARD ·

STATE NATIONAL GUARD
ANNUAL PLATE

HEART OF DIXIE · **Alabama** ·
PEARL HARBOR SURVIVOR
300
MO · · YR

PEARL HARBOR SURVIVORS

HEART OF DIXIE · **Alabama** ·
HS6700
MO · HELPING SCHOOLS · YR

SCHOOL FUND-RAISING
PLATE

HEART OF DIXIE · **AUBURN** · HEART OF DIXIE
UNIVERSITY
1 TIGR
MO · **Alabama** · YR

AUBURN UNIVERSITY
PRESTIGE
(PERSONALIZED COLLEGIATE)

"The Heart of Dixie" issues one fully-reflectorized license plate for all vehicles. A county code system is in use, and all passenger car plates are of the same red, white and blue design. A new multi-year base plate introduced January 1,1992 will replace all previous bases by Dec. 1992.

Distinctive captions:

ANTIQUE VEHICLE - Collector's vehicle 25 years or older.
HELPING SCHOOLS - School fund raising plate.
TRANSIT- Dealer's transit plate

Codes:

Alabama plates have a numeric county prefix.The counties and (county seats) are:

1. Jefferson (Birmingham)
2. Mobile (Mobile)
3. Montgomery (Montgomery)
4. Autauga (Prattville)
5. Baldwin (Bay Minette)
6. Barbour (Clayton)
7. Bibb (Centerville)
8. Blount (Oneonta)
9. Bullock (Union Springs)
10. Butler (Greenville)
11. Calhoun (Anniston)
12. Chambers (Lafayette)
13. Cherokee (Centre)
14. Chilton (Clanton)
15. Choctaw (Butler)
16. Clarke (Grove Hill)
17. Clay (Ashland)
18. Cleburne (Heflin)
19. Coffee (Elba)
20. Colbert (Tuscumbia)
21. Conecuh (Evergreen)
22. Coosa (Rockford)
23. Covington (Audalusia)
24. Crenshaw (Luverne)
25. Cullman (Cullman)
26. Dale (Ozark)
27. Dallas (Selma)
28. DeKalb (Fort Payne)
29. Elmore (Wetumpka)
30. Escambia (Brewton)
31. Etowah(Gadsden)
32. Fayette (Fayette)
33. Franklin (Russellville)
34. Geneva (Geneva)
35. Greene (Eutaw)
36. Hale (Greensboro)
37. Henry (Abbeville)
38. Houston (Dothan)
39. Jackson (Scottsboro)
40. Lamar (Vernon)
41. Lauderdale (Florence)
42. Lawrence (Moulton)
43. Lee (Opelika)
44. Limestone (Athens)
45. Lowndes (Hayneville)46. Macon (Tuskegee)
47. Madison (Huntsville)
48. Marengo (Linden)
49. Marion (Hamilton)
50. Marshall (Guntersville)
51. Monroe (Monroeville)
52. Morgan (Decatur)
53. Perry (Marion)
54. Pickens (Carrollton)
55. Pike (Troy)
56. Randolph (Wedowee)
57. Russell (Phenix City)
58. Shelby (Columbiana)
59. Saint. Clair (Ashville)
60. Sumpter (Livingston)
61. Talladega (Talladega)
62. Tallapoosa Tallapoosa)
63. Tuscaloosa (Tuscaloosa)
64. Walker (Jasper)
65. Washington (Chatom)
66. Wilcox (Camden)
67. Winston (Double Springs)
70. Replacement
80. Supplemental

Alpha prefixes reserved for special use:

BB-60 - Chm. Alabama Battleship Comm.
CO- County owned vehicle
D- Dealer
H- Hearse or ambulance
L-Truck limited to 15 mile use known as "mule tag"
MOH- Medal of Honor recipient
MU- Municipal owned vehicle

POW- Former prisoner of war
PUD- Public utility
RS- Rescue squad
RT- Rental trailer
S- State owned
TR- Trailer
Z- Taxi

Trucks have a numeric county code and a 2 character class and weight code:

Alpha class code   Numeric indicates max. gross wgt. in thousands of pounds

	1	**2**	**3**	**4**	**5**	**6**	**7**	**8**
F-Farm	30	42						
L-Forest prod.	30	42						
X-Truck	12,18	26	33	42	55	73,290	80	over 80

Personalized plates are available for $50 per year additional fee from Motor Vehicle License Division, P.O.Box 104, Montgomery AL 36101. Up to 7 characters permitted.

To trace the owner of a vehicle by the plate- write to:Motor Vehicle License Division, P.O.Box 104, Montgomery AL 36101. Give the plate number and request an abstract of the registration. Fee $.50; certified $1.50.

ALASKA

STATE ROUTE MARKER

ALASKA ★ **7**

FAIRBANKS

ANCHORAGE

KFQD 750 Anchorage
KYAK 650 Anchorage
KCBF 820 Fairbanks

AM RADIO

·ALASKA·
MO YR
CBA 123
· The Last Frontier ·

2 PLATES VALIDATED BY
2 DECALS ON EACH PLATE

MO **·ALASKA·** YR
KENAI
· The Last Frontier ·

PERSONALIZED

MO **·ALASKA·** YR
HCP♿123
· The Last Frontier ·

HANDICAPPED

MO **·ALASKA·** YR
DAV♿123
· DISABLED VET ·

DISABLED VETERAN

·ALASKA·
AST 123
· TROOPER ·

STATE TROOPER

MO **·ALASKA·** YR
3
· LEGISLATOR ·

LEGISLATOR
ALL NUMERICS 3-63

MO **·ALASKA·** YR
FWP 123
· PROTECTION ·

FISH & WILDLIFE
PROTECTION

MO **·ALASKA·** YR
2-123
OFFICIAL USE ONLY

STATE OWNED

MO **·ALASKA·** YR
1001BA

TRUCK

MO **·ALASKA·** YR
1001SA
· COMMERCIAL ·

COMMERCIAL TRAILER

MO **·ALASKA·** YR
3301FA
· FARM ·

FARM VEHICLE

MO **·ALASKA·** YR
YYE123
· EXEMPT ·

CHARITABLE
ORGANIZATION

MO **·ALASKA·**
KL7ABC

AMATUER RADIO

MO **·ALASKA·** YR
POW 055
EX PRISONER OF WAR

EX PRISONER OF WAR

MO **·ALASKA·** YR
PH 117
Pearl Harbor Survivor

PEARL HARBOR SURVIVOR

MO **·ALASKA·** YR
OHV123
· OCCASIONAL ·

OFF HIGHWAY VEHICLE

ALASKA

"The Last Frontier" issues two fully-reflectorized license plates. A three alpha - three numeric format is used for all passenger plates which are on the same blue on gold design.

Distinctive captions:

PROTECTION - Fish and wildlife protection
THE LAST FRONTIER- State slogan on all but special plates
HISTORICAL- A vehicle at least 30 years old
OFFICIAL USE ONLY - State owned vehicle
OCCASIONAL-Off the road vehicle

Codes:

Alaska issues 3 alpha - 3 numeric plates to passenger vehicles and 4 numeric- 2 alpha plates to trucks, trailers and buses.

The following alpha combinations are used to identify classes of vehicles:

Prefix:

AST	Alaska State Troopers
FWP	Fish and wildlife protection
HCP	Handicapped person
KL7,WL7	Ham radio call letters assigned Alaska
YY	Charitable organization
ZZ	For hire vehicle

Suffix:

BA - BP	Truck
DL	Dealer
FA	Farm
PA,PC,PD	Trailer (private)
PB,PH	Non commercial trailer
SA -SD	Commercial trailer

Alaska does not designate county or weight of a vehicle on the license plate.

Personalized plates are available for a one time charge of $30.00 plus the regular fee from Alaska Dept. of Public safety,DMV Special Programs Unit,5700 E. Tudor Rd, Anchorage AK 99507. 2 - 6 alpha and or numeric characters may be requested.

To trace the owner of a vehicle write to Division of Motor Vehicles,2150 E.Dowling Rd., Anchorage 99510. Give the plate or vehicle ID number and request an abstract of the registration. The fee is $5.00 per record. Information is available only by mail. Use this address to request a sample plate.

ARIZONA

STATE ROUTE MARKER

ARIZONA 85

KNIX 1580 Phoenix
KFLT 830 Tucson
KUAT 1550 Tucson
KTKT 990 Tucson

PHOENIX

TUCSON

AM RADIO

MO ARIZONA HBC♣123 **GRAND CANYON STATE YR**
1 PLATE VALIDATED
BY 2 DECALS

MO ARIZONA CACTUS **GRAND CANYON STATE YR**
PERSONALIZED

MO ARIZONA ♿ 0001 **GRAND CANYON STATE YR**
PERMANENT DISABILITY

ARIZONA GA-188AE **STATE VEHICLE**
STATE VEHICLE

ARIZONA PS-1001 **GRAND CANYON STATE**
COUNTY VEHICLE

MO ARIZONA 2AA-001 **GRAND CANYON STATE YR**
COMMERCIAL

MO ARIZONA 2TA-001 **TRUCK TRACTOR YR**
TRUCK TRACTOR

MO ARIZONA 00A♣001 **APPORTIONED YR**
INTERSTATE USE
APPORTIONED

MO ARIZONA K7GNN **GRAND CANYON STATE YR**
AMATEUR RADIO

MO DLR ARIZONA 92 DL-0001 **GRAND CANYON STATE YR**
AUTOMOBLE DEALER
COLORS CHANGE YEARLY
UNLESS EXTENDED BY STICKER

MO • ARIZONA 77 • HISTORIC VEHICLE 77T **GRAND CANYON STATE YR**
HISTORIC VEHICLE
PLATE BASE IS ALL COPPER

MO ARIZONA YR A0001 **Arizona State University**
COLLEGIATE PLATE

MO ARIZONA FORMER P.O.W. A01 **GRAND CANYON STATE YR**
FORMER P.O.W.

MO ARIZONA ★★★ 000 **MEDAL OF HONOR YR**
CONGRESSIONAL
MEDAL OF HONOR
RECIPIENT

ARIZONA MO 0001 **PURPLE HEART YR**
PURPLE HEART MEDAL
RECIPIENT

MO • ARIZONA • YR PEARL HARBOR SURVIVOR 050 **REMEMBER PEARL HARBOR**
PEARL HARBOR
SURVIVOR

14

ARIZONA

"The Grand Canyon State" now issues only one partially reflectorized (glass beads on paint background) license plates for most vehicles, having dropped the two plate requirement. Plates continued to be issued in pairs for: University plates, Medal of Honor, POW's, Pearl Harbor Survivors.

Distinctive captions:

CLASSIC CAR - Vehicle listed by Classic Car Association of America
HISTORIC VEHICLE - A collectors vehicle at least 25 years old
HORSELESS CARRIAGE - A vehicle manufactured 1915 or earlier.
NON COMMERCIAL - Pickup truck not used for commercial purposes.
(This plate is no longer issued, but is still valid.
Saguaro cactus is the state symbol and appears
in the center of the white on maroon passenger plate. ---->

Codes:

Arizona issues 3 alpha-3 numeric character plates to regular passenger vehicles. This numbering system is used for individual vehicle identification only, and does not contain any county of origin, occupation or other hidden codes. Only 1 plate is now required to be displayed, although earlier issues were in pairs.

Commercial vehicle plates have 6 characters :
1 **AB** -123 1 numeric - 2 alpha - 3 numeric
1 **ZA** -123 Bus and taxi plates display **Z** in first alpha position
1 **X A** -123 Trucks operating interstate display **X** as first alpha.
1 **TA** -123 Truck tractors display **T** as first alpha.

Prefixes can also be used for identification on older issue plates

AZ - Dept. of Public Safety	**ST / SA** - State of Arizona
DL- Automobile dealer	**TR** - Trailer dealer
ED- School vehicle	**XP** - Transporter
H - Hearing impaired	**Z** - Proportional trailer

Individual government agency - designating plates are no longer issued but remain valid. New plates display **G** plus 3 numeric - 2 alpha.

All other classes of Arizona plates are easily identified by captions that appear on the plate.

Personalized plates are available from Motor Vehicle Division, Special Plate Section Box 2100 mail drop 506m, Phoenix 85001. The fee is $25.00 plus additional $10 per year renewal fee. 2 - 6 characters are permitted. Collegiate personalized initial fee is $50 and $35 annual renewal in addition to regular registration fees..

To trace the owner of an Arizona vehicle through the plate number should be done through law enforcement agencies. Public access to Motor Vehicle Dept records is restricted by a law passed in 1981. For details write to Arizona Motor Vehicle Division, records section, Box 2100 mail drop 504m Phoenix AZ 85001

ARKANSAS

STATE
ROUTE MARKER

5

★ **KAAY 1090** Little Rock
KBIS 1010 Little Rock
KFAY 1030 Farmington

FARMINGTON

LITTLE ROCK

AM RADIO

RRR 140
The Natural State
1 PLATE VALIDATED
BY 2 DECALS

FBC 123
Land of Opportunity
PASSENGER PLATE
OLDER ISSUE

JWR
The Natural State
PERSONALIZED

GBC 123
HANDICAPPED ISSUED
REGULAR PLATE
ISA DECAL OPTIONAL

FIW 607
OFFICIAL BUSINESS ONLY
STATE OWNED VEHICLE

AUV 797
PUBLIC PROPERTY
COUNTY AND CITY
OWNED VEHICLE

DAV-1099
DISABLED VETERAN
DISABLED VETERAN

PXN 405
FARM TO MARKET
FARM TO MARKET
BUS

AUS 199
B S & O
BOY SCOUT
AND ORPHANAGE BUS

M5
DEALER
AUTO MASTER DEALER

D 580
TRUCK EXP.
TRUCK AND
TRUCK TRACTOR
(COLORS REVERSE YEARLY)

ST 74474
EXP. 6-30-
SEMI-TRAILER
(COLORS REVERSE YEARLY)

430
ANTIQUE CAR
ARKANSAS
HISTORIC OR
SPECIAL INTEREST

PHS 044
Pearl Harbor Survivor
PEARL HARBOR SURVIVOR

000188
U.S. ARMED FORCES RETIRED
RETIRED MILITARY

MH2
CONGRESSIONAL
MEDAL OF HONOR
VALOR ABOVE AND BEYOND THE CALL OF DUTY
CONGRESSIONAL
MEDAL OF HONOR
RECIPIENT

"The Natural State" issues one fully-reflectorized license plate for passenger vehicles. Many of the non-passenger and annual plates are not reflectorized. The earlier issued "Land of Opportunity" plates are now being phased out.

Distinctive captions:
ARK NG--Arkansas National Guard
BS&O - Boy scout and orphanage bus
BORDER CITY - Taxi licensed to operate in limited area across state line
FARM PRODUCTS - Farm truck
FARM-TO-MARKET -Bus limited to operation between farm and market
PUBLIC PROPERTY - City or county owned vehicle

Codes:
Passenger cars and pickup trucks are issued 3 alpha-3 numeric plates. Truck and trailer plates have 1 or 2 alpha prefix followed by numerics. The prefixes have the following meanings:

Passenger car
DAV -Disabled veteran
EX -Extra dealer plate
F -Franchise dealer
M - Master dealer

MF - Master Manufacturer
MX - Manufacturer
  (extra plate)
POW- Ex prisoner of
  War

PH - Purple Heart
  recipient
PHS - Pearl Harbor
  survivor

Trucks and trailers:

B	Truck 6,001 - 19,000 lbs gross loaded weight
C	Truck 20,001 - 39,000 lbs gross loaded weight
D	Truck 40,001 - 55,000 lbs gross loaded weight
E	Truck 56,001 - 59,000 lbs gross loaded weight
H	Truck 60,001 - 67,000 lbs gross loaded weight
J	Truck 68,001 - 73,000 lbs gross loaded weight
NR	Vehicle transporting natural resources (forest products clay etc.)
ST	Semi-trailer
T	Full trailer
X	County or city owned truck
K	Truck 73,281 - 87,000 lbs gross loaded weight

NR or Farm plates:

A	8,000 -17,000 lbs gross loaded weight
B	3 or more axles

Trailers:

B over **T**	Boat trailer
G over **T**	Goose neck trailer
ST	Semi-trailer

Arkansas does not identify the county of origin by any code on the plate.

Personalized plates are available for $25.00 above normal fee from Motor Vehicle Division Box 1272, Little Rock 72203. Up to 7 alpha numeric characters can be requested.

To trace the owner of a vehicle send the plate number to Motor Vehicle Div., Box 1272 Little Rock AR 72203 and request an abstract of the registration. The fee is $1.00 per inquiry.Questionable inquiries may be referred to law enforcement agency.

CALIFORNIA

★ **KNBR 680** San Francisco
★ **KGO 810** San Francisco
★ **KFBK 1530** Sacramento
★ **KNX 1070** Los Angeles
★ **KFI 640** Los Angeles

AM RADIO

STATE ROUTE MARKER

CALIFORNIA 2ABC123

2 PERMANENT PLATES
VALIDATED BY 2 DECALS
ON REAR PLATE
1988-PRESENT

CALIFORNIA ABC123

PASSENGER OLDER ISSUE
1963-1969

CALIFORNIA 123 ABC

PASSENGER OLDER ISSUE
1970-1986

CALIFORNIA 2ABC123
The Golden State

PASSENGER OLDER ISSUE
1987

CALIFORNIA THURZ
1984 OLYMPICS

1984 OLYMPIC GAMES
PERSONALIZED

CALIFORNIA CAJUN
Share the Olympic Victory

OLYMPIC TRAINING
PERSONALIZED

CALIFORNIA SURFSUP

ENVIRONMENTAL
(PERSONALIZED)

CALIFORNIA 1234 US
1791 • BILL OF RIGHTS • 1991

BILL OF RIGHTS
COMMEMORATIVE PLATE

CALIFORNIA E 400049

STATE OWNED VEHICLE

CALIFORNIA E 462001

CITY/COUNTY/GOVT
VEHICLE

CALIFORNIA 3A12345

COMMERCIAL VEHICLE
(TRUCK)

CALIFORNIA 1UC1575

TRAILER

CALIFORNIA 9999PH
COMBAT WOUNED

PURPLE HEART RECIPIENT

CALIFORNIA S 2 s

STATE SENATE
SMALL "S" INDICATES
SECOND CAR

CALIFORNIA 0001

PRESS
PHOTOGRAPHER

CALIFORNIA CONSTABLE 123

COUNTY PEACE
OFFICER

CALIFORNIA

"The Golden State" has not had a complete general plate re-issue since 1963, and four different bases are currently in use. Plates are issued in pairs, and fully reflectorized plates were first issued in 1982. Special plates to commemorate the 1984 Olympics and the U.S. Olympic Training Center have been issued and remain valid.

Distinctive captions:

DISMANTLER- Plate to move vehicle to a place of dismantling (junk yard).
HISTORICAL- A vehicle manufactured after 1922 and at least 25 years old.
HORSELESS CARRIAGE- 16 cyl. engine pre 1965, or veh mfg.before 1923.

⬦ E - State owned　⬠ E - City/Cnty U.S. Govt　△ Pp - Press Photographer

Codes:

California issues 6 character (3 alpha-3 numeric; 3 numeric - 3 alpha) and 7 character(1 numeric-3 alpha-3 numeric plates. Several graphic design base plates are in use. Commercial vehicle plates have 1 alpha-6 numeric plates where the alpha appears in different positions. The following alpha prefixes are reserved for special group:

A- State assemblyman
AA - Assemblyman's personal **vehicle**
AA-TZ- Trailer not subject to wgt.fee
DV -Disabled veteran

S- State senator
Ss- Senator's personal vehicle
SR- Retired senator

California does not indicate county of origin or weight of vehicle on plates. California old car enthusiasts are able to register their 1962 or earlier vehicles with a matched pair of original California plates of the year the car was manufactured.

Personalized plates(called Environmental plates in California) are available at all Dept. of Motor Vehicle offices. 2-7 alpha numeric characters will be considered. Initial fee $40; $25 annual renewal fee in addition to the regular registration fees.

To trace the owner of a California registered vehicle one must go through a law enforcement or other qualified agency. Motor vehicle registration information is no longer available to the general public. Samples from DMV P.O.Box 932345 Sacramento.

COLORADO

2 PLATES VALIDATED BY
2 DECALS ON REAR PLATE

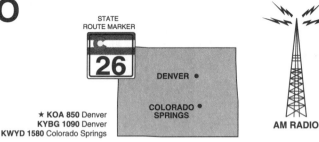

STATE
ROUTE MARKER

26

★ **KOA 850** Denver
KYBG 1090 Denver
KWYD 1580 Colorado Springs

DENVER ●

COLORADO ●
SPRINGS

AM RADIO

PASSENGER, REGULAR
ALSO 2 ALPHA -
1, 2, 3, 4 NUMERIC

DESIGNER PLATE
$25 FEE

PERSONALIZED

DISABLED

DISABLED VETERAN

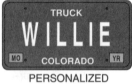

PERSONALIZED
TRUCK

COUNTY VEHICLE

CITY VEHICLE CITY NAME
ON REAR PLATE

TRUCK TRACTOR

TRUCK GVW GROSS
VEHICLE COMBINED
WEIGHT OF TRUCK & LOAD

INTERSTATE TRUCK
APPORTIONED

PURPLE HEART RECIPIENT

COLLECTOR

PEARL HARBOR
SURVIVOR

FORMER PRISONER
OF WAR

Colorado issues two partially-reflectorized (glass beads on paint) white on green plates. These plates contain a county code numbering system. Colorful blue on white "designer" plates are available for an additional fee.

Distinctive captions:

COLLECTORS SERIES -Vehicle 25 years or older

DEPOT - Used by dealers to move a vehicle.

Codes:

All private and commercial license plates have an alpha prefix that indicates the county of origin and (county seat) as follows:

Old code	New code	County	County seat	Old code	New code	County	County seat
AA-GN	AAA-DZZ	Denver	Denver				
GP-HX	VEC-VVC	Pueblo	Pueblo	XP-XR	UBL-UCA	Lincoln	Hugo
HY-JW	WAA-WNK	Weld	Greeley	XS-XT	EPB-EPU	Elbert	Kiowa
JX-LL	KAA-LZZ	El Paso	Colo. Springs	XU-XV	VYP-VZA	Saguache	Saguache
LM-LT	UAA-UBK	Las Animas	Trinidad	XW-XX	EET-EFA	Crowley	Ordway
LU-MK	FHA-FZZ	Larimer	Ft. Collins	XY-XZ	VBB-VBR	Phillips	Holyoke
ML-NF	MAA-NZZ	Boulder	Boulder	YA-YA	EEL-EES	Costilla	San Luis
NH-NZ	UEJ-UNL	Mesa	Grand Junction	YB-YC	WNL-WNY	Sedgwick	Julesburg
PA-PG	UXS-UZZ	Otero	LaJunta	YD-YE	EYC-EZC	Gunnison	Gunnison
PH-RP	PAA-RZZ	Arapahoe	Littleton	YF-YH	FCD-FDE	Lake	Leadville
RS-TD	GAA-JZZ	Jefferson	Golden	YJ-YK	UNS-UPX	Moffat	Craig
TE-UF	SAA-TZZ	Adams	Brighton	YL-YL	WRN-WSR	Teller	Cripple Creek
UG-UN	UCB-EUH	Logan	Sterling	YM-YN	EMB-EPA	Eagle	Eagle
UP-UV	EPV-ETV	Fremont	Canon City	YP-YP	WUS-WUY	Kiowa	Eads
UW-VD	UVA-UXR	Morgan	Ft. Morgan	YR-YR	ECM-ECT	Cheyenne	Cheyenne Wells
VE-VF	EZF-EZW	Huerfano	Walsenburg	YS-YT	EHW-EMA	Douglas	Castle Rock
VG-VK	VDN-VEY	Prowers	Lamar	YU-YU	FAA-FAL	Archuleta	Pagosa Springs
VL-VR	EFH-EHP	Delta	Delta	YU-YW	VVD-VVV	Rio Blanco	Meeker
VS-VU	WTL-WUR	Yuma	Yuma	YX-YX	VZF-VZR	San Miguel	Telluride
VV-WA	FDF-FGB	La Plata	Durango	YY-YZ	ECU-EDU	Clear Creek	Georgetown
WB-WF	USM-UUZ	Montrose	Montrose	ZA-ZA	EFB-EFG	Custer	Westcliffe
WG-WH	EBE-EBW	Baca	Springfield	ZB-ZC	EWZ-EYB	Grand	Hot Sulfur Spgs.
WJ-WL	VVW-VWZ	Rio Grande	Del Norte	ZD-ZD	VAH-VBA	Park	Fairplay
WM-WR	ETW-EWM	Garfield	Glenwood Spgs.	ZE-ZE	VZB-VZE	San Juan	Silverton
WS-WT	EDV-EEK	Conejos	Conejos	ZF-ZF	VAA-VAG	Ouray	Ouray
WU-WV	WUZ-WVV	Kit Carson	Burlington	ZG, ZP	VBS-VDM	Pitkin	Aspen
WW-WY	WST-WTK	Washington	Akron	ZH-ZH	EHR-EHV	Dolores	Dove Creek
WZ-XB	VXA-VYN	Routt	Steamboat Spgs.	ZJ-ZJ	FGC-FGH	Jackson	Walden
XC-XD	EBX-ECL	Bent	Las Animas	ZK-ZK	EWN-EWV	Gilpin	Central City
XG-XE	EAA-EBD	Alamosa	Alamosa	ZL,ZR	WNZ-WRM	Summit	Breckenridge
XH-XK	FAM-FCC	Chaffee	Salida	ZM-ZM	UNM-UNR	Mineral	Creede
XL-XN	UPY-USL	Montezuma	Cortez	ZN-ZN	EZD-EZE	Hinsdale	Lake City

Other codes:

CC - Honorary Consul

MC - Member of Congress

S.M.E - Special mobil equipment

USS 1 and **2** - U.S.Senators

ZAA - (Z plus 2 alpha) prefix - Rental car

ZA - (Z plus 1 alpha) prefix - Is not a rental

Colorado does not designate the weight of a vehicle on the plate.

Personalized plates are available from Colorado Dept of Revenue 140 W 6th Ave, Denver 80204. The extra fee is $35 and $25 to renew. 2-6 alpha numeric characters are permitted. The local name for these tags is "Pothole plates", because the sales revenue is used for road maintenance.

To trace the owner of a Colorado registered vehicle write to Dept. of Revenue, Motor Vehicle Master Files Section, 140 W. 6th Ave., Denver 80204. Give them the plate number and request an abstract of the registration. The fee is $2.00.

CONNECTICUT

STATE ROUTE MARKER

99

★ **WTIC 1080** Hartford
WDRC 1360 Hartford
WPOP 1410 Hartford

HARTFORD

AM RADIO

CONNECTICUT MO YR
123·ABC
CON STITUTION STATE

2 PLATES VALIDATED BY 1
DECAL ON REAR PLATE
1988 ISSUE

CONNECTICUT MO YR
NUTMEG
CON STITUTION STATE

PERSONALIZED

CONNECTICUT MO YR
124·CZE
.COMBINATION.

COMBINATION BUSINESS
AND PRIVATE USE
(CAN BE ALL NUMERIC)

CONNECTICUT MO YR
697·G
CON STITUTION STATE

HANDICAPPED

CONNECTICUT MO YR
641·C
.COMBINATION.

BUSINESS & PRIVATE
HANDICAPPED VEHICLE

CON STITUTION STATE
AB·1234
CONNECTICUT MO YR

PASSENGER (1 PLATE)
SEVERAL OLDER PLATES
1976-1987 STILL IN USE

CONNECTICUT
U·2
.HEARSE. MO YR

HEARSE

CONNECTICUT MO YR
H·62005
.COMBINATION.

COMMERICAL VEHICLE
(2 PLATES)

CONNECTICUT MO YR
1635·AT
.APPORTIONED.

INTERSTATE TRAILER
APPORTIONED

CONNECTICUT MO YR
1001·A
.APPORTIONED.

INTERSTATE VEHICLE
APPORTIONED

CONNECTICUT MO YR
12· N Y P
CON STITUTION STATE

NEW YORK PRESS

CONNECTICUT MO YR
123· C N P
CON STITUTION STATE

CONNECTICUT NEWS
PHOTOGRAPHER

CONNECTICUT MO YR
1·123
STATE

STATE OWNED
PREFIX INDICATES DEPT.

CONNECTICUT MO YR
K1⚡ABC
CON STITUTION STATE

HAM RADIO

CONNECTICUT MO YR
MD·1234
CON STITUTION STATE

MEDICAL DOCTOR

3458 E A
CONN MO-YR

COLLECTOR
EARLY AMERICAN

CONNECTICUT

"The Constitution State" issues two partially-reflectorized (glass beads on paint) license plates. There has not been a general re-issue of plates since 1957, so numerous older bases are still in use, with many motorists displaying only a rear plate.

Distinctive captions:

CONSTITUTION STATE - Connecticut's colonial government served as a model for the U.S. Constitution.

COMBINATION - Vehicle used for both private and commercial purposes.

EXP TEST-Plate used to test experimental vehicles

FARM - Vehicle transporting farm prod. or livestock-limited highway use.

LIVERY - Passenger vehicle for hire, other than taxi or bus.

REPAIR - Plate issued to persons engaged in motor vehicle repair.

SERV. BUS - Vehicle used to transport 8 or more people without charge.

TRANS.- Transporter plate.

VETERAN- Disabled veteran

VAN POOL- -Commuter van

Codes:

Most Connecticut passenger plates have 3 numeric - 3 alpha characters. However, since 1957-74plain blue, 1974-76 blue on white, 1976-87 slogan blue and 1988 map blue plates are still in use, various alpha/numeric combinations can be observed.

Commercial vehicle plates have 1 alpha-5 numeric characters.The following alpha characters are reserved for special use:

AL- American Legion
ARC- American Red Cross
CNP- Conn. news photographer
DA - DZ - Used car dealer
DV - Disabled veteran
MD- Medical doctor
NYP- New York Press

U- Hearse
VFW - Veterans organization
YD - Yankee Division
X,XA-XZ- New car dealer
S- Special equipment dealer
**RA - RZ - ** - Repair

License plates are revalidated every two years by a decal. The schedule is based on the first letter of the owner's last name.

INITIAL	RENEWAL MO.	INITIAL	RENEWAL MO
A-B	MAY	M-O	NOVEMBER
C	JUNE	P-R	DECEMBER
D-F	AUGUST	S	JANUARY
G-J	SEPTEMBER	T-Z	FEBRUARY
K,L,N	OCTOBER		

Commercial- April
combination - July
Miscellaneous - March

The alpha suffix on municipal plates are the initials of the city or town. Plate numbers 1-5,000 are assigned by the Commissioner of Motor Vehicles. Connecticut does not indicate county of origin or weight of a vehicle on the plate.

Personalized plates write to Commissioner of Motor Vehicles, 60 State St. Weathersfield CT.06109.Enclose $47.00 check. If available, plate will be ordered. When delivered, an additional $4.00 is required. A maximum of 6 characters allowed.

To trace the owner of a Connecticut vehicle, send a written request to the Commissioner of Motor Vehicles in Weathersfield .The fee is $.50 per record.

DELAWARE

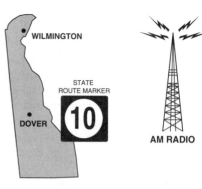

WDEL 1150 Wilmington
WDOV 1410 Dover
WKEN 1600 Dover

WILMINGTON

DOVER

STATE
ROUTE MARKER

10

AM RADIO

1 PLATE VALIDATED
BY 1 DECAL

PASSENGER
OLDER ISSUE

PASSENGER (1951 ISSUE)
STANLESS STEEL
RIVITED NUMBERS
SCOTCH LIGHT COATING

PASSENGER (1947 ISSUE)
STAINLESS STEEL
RIVITED NUMBERS

PORCELAIN PLATE
ORIGNAL PRE-WAR ISSUE
STILL AVAILABLE AS
SPECIAL ORDER

PERSONALIZED

HANDICAPPED

STATE OWNED

PLEASURE- COMMERCIAL
(STATION WAGON)

COMMERCIAL

TRAILER

FARM TRUCK

DEALER

INITIALS - JUDGE

INITIALS - STATE REP.

INITIALS - STATE SENATOR

24

"The First State" issues one fully-reflectorized license plate for all vehicles. Delaware's plates are unique because they are neither embossed or debossed. They are made with a silk-printing process and are completely flat. Replacements for lost, stolen, or damaged plates have the numerics attached by rivets

Distinctive captions:

THE FIRST STATE- Delaware was the first state to ratify the Constitution.
STREET ROD - Modified antique vehicle manufactured prior to 1949

Codes:

Delaware does not designate county of origin or weight of a vehicle on license plates. Regular passenger plates are all numeric. Alpha prefixes indicate classes of vehicles as follows:

A	Ambulance	MIA	Missing in action
C	Commercial vehicle	MOP	Moped
CL	Commercial vehicle	NG	National Guard
CT	Construction equipment	PC	Pleasure / commercial
D	Dealer	POW	Former prisoner of war
DAV	Disabled veteran	R	Rescue vehicle
F	Farm tractor	RF	Armed forces reserves
FD	Fire Dept	RV	Recreational vehicle
FT	Farm truck	T	Trailer
MC	Motorcycle		

Delaware passenger vehicle license plates (except PC) are all numeric. The numbers are the same as the vehicle identification numbers, and the plates stay with the vehicle when ownership changes. To get a particular plate number one must own or scrap the vehicle, and as a result , low license plate numbers are bought and sold on the open market.

Elected officials can use their initials on special state seal plates , however the original number plate must be in the vehicle at all times. These special plates must be removed when the owner leaves office, and the original plates re-attached or surrendered in exchange for personalized.

Delaware permits low number (under 87,000) plates to be re-manufactured in black and white porcelain for use on any passenger or commercial vehicle(except PC plates). These plates must display a current validation decal.

Personalized plates are available through any Motor Vehicle Division office. The fee is $28.75 per year in addition to the regular registration fee. 1-6 alpha or alpha followed by numeric characters can be requested.

To trace the owner of a vehicle registered in Delaware, write to Motor Vehicle Division, Registration Section Box 698, Dover 19903. Give them the plate number and request an abstract of the registration. The fee is $4.00 per record requested. Checks should be made payable to Motor Vehicle Division.

DISTRICT OF COLUMBIA

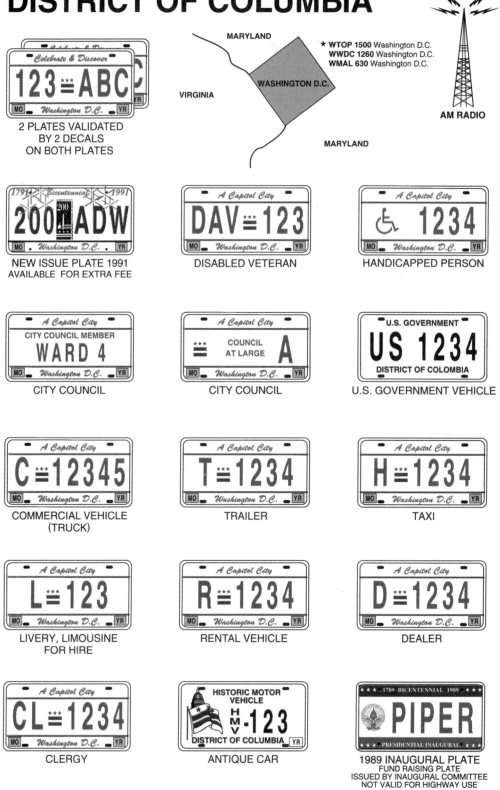

2 PLATES VALIDATED BY 2 DECALS ON BOTH PLATES

MARYLAND
VIRGINIA
WASHINGTON D.C.
MARYLAND

★ **WTOP 1500** Washington D.C.
WWDC 1260 Washington D.C.
WMAL 630 Washington D.C.

AM RADIO

NEW ISSUE PLATE 1991
AVAILABLE FOR EXTRA FEE

DISABLED VETERAN

HANDICAPPED PERSON

CITY COUNCIL

CITY COUNCIL

U.S. GOVERNMENT VEHICLE

COMMERCIAL VEHICLE
(TRUCK)

TRAILER

TAXI

LIVERY, LIMOUSINE
FOR HIRE

RENTAL VEHICLE

DEALER

CLERGY

ANTIQUE CAR

1989 INAUGURAL PLATE
FUND RAISING PLATE
ISSUED BY INAUGURAL COMMITTEE
NOT VALID FOR HIGHWAY USE

26

The "Capital City" issues two fully-reflectorized red white and blue license plates. Low number plates are assigned annually by the mayor's office. A new slogan, "Celebrate and Discover" is being phased in.

Distinctive captions:
All words embossed on District of Columbia plates are self-explanatory.

Codes:
Regular passenger vehicle license plates have 6 numeric characters. Trucks, trailers, and bus plates have an alpha prefix followed by numerics. The following alpha prefixes have special meaning:

B- Bus
C- Commercial vehicle
D- Dealer
DAV- Disabled American veteran
GVT- District of Columbia Government
H- Taxi (H for hire)
H over P- Handicapped person
L- Limousine, livery
MD- Medical doctor
R- Rented vehicle
T- Trailer
TRP- Transporter

District of Columbia does not indicate the weight class or use restrictions of a vehicle on the license plate.

Personalized plates are available from Motor Vehicle Services, 301 C St NW, Washington DC- 20001. 5 or 6 alpha and or numeric characters allowed. Initial fee $25; $10 annual renewal.

To trace the owner of a vehicle, write the Bureau of Motor Vehicles at the above address. Enclose a statement of the reason for this request and a $2.00 fee payable to:District of Columbia Treasurer.

FLORIDA

WJGC 1530 Jacksonville
WINZ 940 Miami
WWFE 670 Miami
WQYK 1010 Tampa
WCOA 1370 Pensacola

STATE ROUTE MARKER
67

AM RADIO

MO FLORIDA YR
JUR 79R
ALACHUA

1 PLATE VALIDATED
BY 2 DECALS
1992 ISSUE

MO FLORIDA YR
FAA 12A
ORANGE

PASSENGER, LIGHT TRUCKS
AND MOTOR COACHES
1986 TO 1991

FLORIDA
ABC 123
MO Challenger YR

CHALLENGER
MEMORIAL PLATE

FLORIDA
MELANIE
MO Challenger YR

CHALLENGER PLATE
PERSONALIZED

MO FLORIDA YR
0001
DMV

HANDICAPPED

FLORIDA
SHERIFF 0001
DMV

COUNTY SHERIFF

FLORIDA
DC 0001
DMV

STATE VEHICLE
DEPT. OF CORRECTION

MO FLORIDA YR
H0001A
DMV

TRUCKS OVER 5000LBS.
BUSES, WRECKERS

MO FLORIDA YR
G0001A
DMV

GOAT TRUCKS ISSUED FOR
VEHICLES USED BY A FARMER
HARVESTING A CROP

MO FLORIDA YR
PAA Columbus JUBILEE 123
1492-1992
THE
QUINCENTENNIAL STATE

QUINCENTENNIAL PLATE

MO FLORIDA YR
A00001A
APPORTIONED

APPORTIONED TRUCK OR
TRACTOR INTERSTATE USE

MO FLORIDA YR
SEMINOLE 123
INDIAN

SEMINOLE INDIAN
TRIBE MEMBER

MO FLORIDA YR
65274
UNIVERSITY OF CENTRAL FLORIDA

COLLEGIATE PLATE

FLORIDA
MEDAL OF HONOR 0
DMV

CONGRESSIONAL
MEDAL OF HONOR
RECIPIENT

MO FLORIDA YR
TCM 011
PANTHER

SAVE THE FLORIDA
PANTHER PLATE

MO FLORIDA YR
HAA 123
Save the Manatee

SAVE THE MANATEE
PLATE

28

"The Sunshine State" issues one full-reflectorized license plate. All regular passenger plates display the county name. Florida has demonstrated that special license plates can be an excellent fundraising source having raised millions to: save the manatee, Florida panther and memorialize the Challenger.

Distinctive captions:

HORSELESS CARRIAGE - An exhibition vehicle 35 yrs old
INDEFINITE - Permanent rental trailer registration
LEASE - Vehicle operated under lease from the owner
STREET ROD - Pre 1949 modified exhibit vehicle

Codes:

The Florida numbering system is as follows:
Previous passenger, motor coach, light trucks: 3 alpha - 3 numeric and
4 alpha- 2 numeric. Currently it is 3 alpha - 2 numeric -1 alpha (ABC-12A).
Trucks, tractors, ambulance, vehicles used as tools: Always have 6 characters
1 or 2 alpha prefix- numerics-1 alpha suffix.
The letter "O" does not appear in the third position on passenger plates or the second alpha position on non-passenger plates. Numerics begin with 001,0001, and 00001.
The county of origin appears at the bottom of all plates issued since 1980, except for permanent plates. DMV indicates Division of Motor Vehicles and is used instead of the county name on special plates.

The following prefixes are reserved for special use:

ACS - Agriculture Consumer Svcs.
DC - Dept. of Corrections
DDL- Div. of Drivers Licensing
DMV - Div. of Motor Vehicles
DNR - Div. Natural Resources
DOT - Dept.. of Transportation
DV - Disabled Veteran
FBC - Florida Board of Conservation
FDC - Florida Dept..of Commerce
FFS - Florida Forest Service
FHP- Florida Highway Patrol
FIC - Florida Industrial Commission
FMP - Florida Marine Patrol

FPS - Florida Park Service
GFC - Game and Fish Commission
HP- Handicapped person
M plus 2 alphas- Dealers
MC - Member of Congress
MF- Franchised vehicle dealer
PP - Harvest truck
PRESS - Members of the press
PSC - Public Service Commission
USS - U.S. Senator
X - Exempt from registration fee
YAA - **ZZZ** Rental or Lease vehicle

Personalized plates are available from any Motor Vehicle Dept. Office. Up to 7 alpha and numeric characters allowed. Fee is $12. The Manatee, Panther and collegiate plates cost $27.Fees are in addition to registration cost.

To trace the owner of vehicle write to Florida Dept. of Safety,Div. of Motor Vehicles, Neil Kirkman Bldg., Tallahassee FL 32399. Give the plate number and request an abstract of the registration.The fee is fifty cents per request. Use this address for samples

GEORGIA

STATE ROUTE MARKER

32

ATLANTA
MACON

★ WSB 750 Atlanta
WGST 640 Atlanta
WGUN 1010 Atlanta
WMAZ 940 Macon

AM RADIO

19 • Georgia • YR
ABC 123
CLAYTON
1 PLATE VALIDATED
BY 1 YEAR DECAL

19 • Georgia • YR
PEACH
WASHINGTON
PERSONALIZED

19 • Georgia • YR
1234
WASHINGTON
DISABLED

19 • Georgia • YR
HONORARY CONSUL 123
CHATTAHOOCHEE
HONORARY CONSUL

19 • Georgia • YR
STATE GOVT 1234
HENRY
STATE/COUNTY/CITY
DECAL FOR GOVT. BRANCH

19 • Georgia • YR
US 12
CONGRESSMAN
U.S. CONGRESSMAN

19 • Georgia • YR
12 34
REPRESENTATIVE
STATE REPRESENTATIVE

19 • Georgia • YR
SHERIFF 12
CLAYTON
SHERIFF

19 • Georgia • YR
JN1234
FULTON
TRUCKS & TRACTORS
18,001-16,000LBS

• GEORGIA •
HH1234
19   92
TRUCKS FOR HIRE 36-40,000LB
COLORS CHANGE YEARLY

19 GEORGIA 92
P 12345
IRP
INTERSTATE TRUCK
NOT FOR HIRE

19 GEORGIA 92
C 12345
IRP
INTERSTATE TRACTOR
FOR HIRE

19 • Georgia • YR
U.S. RESERVE 000
UNION
RESERVE MEMBER

19 • Georgia • YR
1234
GEORGIA TECH
NATIONAL GUARD

19 • Georgia • YR
GT 1234
GEORGIA TECH
COLLEGIATE PLATE
"A RAMBLING WRECK"

19 • Georgia • YR
FOREIGN GOVERNMENT 123
LIBERTY
FOREIGN GOVERNMENT
OWNED VEHICLE

The "Peach State" issues one fully-reflectorized license plate with a uniform format and color scheme for each vehicle. Passenger plates display the county name on a decal. Collegiate plates are available for over 20 colleges and universities.

Distinctive captions:

HISTORICAL VEHICLE: Vehicle at least 30 years old.
LIMITED- Bus operating to and from a military reservation
50 MILE- Bus limited to 50 mile operating radius.
UNL- Unlimited bus licensed to operate throughout state.

Codes:

Georgia issues passenger vehicles 3 alpha-3 numeric semi-permanent (5 year) plates, and is the only state not to have a statewide staggered revalidation system. All passenger plates expire on May 1st. The county of origin appears on the bottom of the plate. The alpha prefixes are:

AAA- SZZ

Trucks and truck tractor plates have a 2 alpha weight class code prefix followed by numerics. Vehicles up to 26,000 lbs. gross weight receive 5 year plates. Vehicles over 26,000 lbs are registered as intrastate Georgia, and interstate operation under the IRP. Intra-state vehicles are registered with annual plates and color combinations change yearly.

The prefixes are as follows:

AA-BZ	Auto and house trailers less than 1000 lbs and all farm trailers
CA-CZ	Auto and house trailers more than 1000 lbs.
EA, FA, FB	Forest products truck
HB	Hearse and ambulances
HF	Trucks and tractors for hire 26,001 - 30,000 lbs.
HG	Truck and truck tractors for hire 30,001 - 36,000 lbs.
HH	Trucks and truck tractors for hire 36,001 - 44,000 lbs.
HI	Trucks and tractors for hire 44,001 - 54,999 lbs.
HJ	Trucks and tractors for hire 55,000 - 63,280 lbs.
HK	Trucks and tractors for hire 63,281 - maximum wgt.
JA- JM	Trucks and tractors 14,001 - 18,000 lbs.
JN- JZ	Trucks and tractors 18,001 - 26,000 lbs.
PF	Trucks and tractors not for hire 26,001 - 30,000 lbs.
PG	Trucks and tractors not for hire 30,001 - 36,000 lbs.
PH	Trucks and tractors not for hire 36,000 - 44,000 lbs.
PI	Trucks and tractors not for hire 44,001 - 54,999 lbs.
PJ	Trucks and tractors not for hire 55,000 - 63,280 lbs.
PK	Trucks and tractors not for hire 63,280 - maximum wgt.
QA- TZ	Trucks and tractors and farm trucks less than 6,000 lbs.
WA- WZ	Trucks and tractors and farm trucks 6,001 - 10,000 lbs.
XA	Trucks and tractors and farm trucks 10,001 - 14,000 lbs.

Bus plates are annual and the alpha prefix indicates the weight class

A - Not over 10,000 lbs, B - 10,000 - 15,000 lbs., C - 15,001 - 20,000 lbs. . D - over 20,000 bs. Georgia became a member of International Registration Plan on Jan 1, 1991, and issues annual apportioned plates. Colors change yearly and have the following codes:P- Not for hire , C- For hire, T- Trailers.

Personalized plate forms available at county courthouse. Send form between May 1 -July 31 to Motor Vehicle Div, Trinity-Washington Bldg.,Atlanta 30334. Fee is $25 plus the regular registration. 1 - 6 characters -5 yr. plate.

To trace the owner of a Georgia registered vehicle one must request the information through law enforcement or other specified agencies. The general public is not permitted access to motor vehicle registration records. Georgia does not offer sample plates.

HAWAII

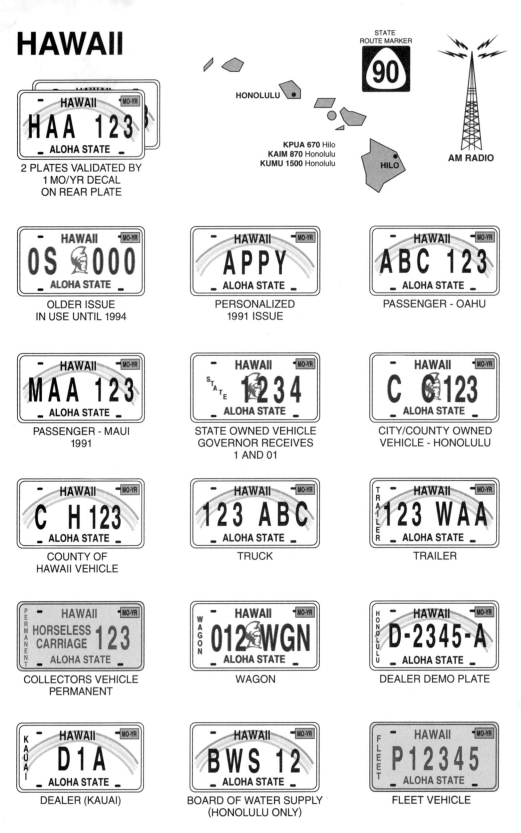

STATE ROUTE MARKER
90

HONOLULU

KPUA 670 Hilo
KAIM 870 Honolulu
KUMU 1500 Honolulu

HILO

AM RADIO

HAWAII — MO-YR
HAA 123
ALOHA STATE

2 PLATES VALIDATED BY
1 MO/YR DECAL
ON REAR PLATE

HAWAII — MO-YR
0S 000
ALOHA STATE

OLDER ISSUE
IN USE UNTIL 1994

HAWAII — MO-YR
APPY
ALOHA STATE

PERSONALIZED
1991 ISSUE

HAWAII — MO-YR
ABC 123
ALOHA STATE

PASSENGER - OAHU

HAWAII — MO-YR
MAA 123
ALOHA STATE

PASSENGER - MAUI
1991

HAWAII — MO-YR
STATE 1234
ALOHA STATE

STATE OWNED VEHICLE
GOVERNOR RECEIVES
1 AND 01

HAWAII — MO-YR
C 6123
ALOHA STATE

CITY/COUNTY OWNED
VEHICLE - HONOLULU

HAWAII — MO-YR
C H 123
ALOHA STATE

COUNTY OF
HAWAII VEHICLE

HAWAII — MO-YR
123 ABC
ALOHA STATE

TRUCK

HAWAII — MO-YR
TRAILER 123 WAA
ALOHA STATE

TRAILER

PERMANENT HAWAII — MO-YR
HORSELESS CARRIAGE 123
ALOHA STATE

COLLECTORS VEHICLE
PERMANENT

WAGON HAWAII — MO-YR
012 WGN
ALOHA STATE

WAGON

HONOLULU HAWAII — MO-YR
D-2345-A
ALOHA STATE

DEALER DEMO PLATE

KAUAI HAWAII — MO-YR
D 1 A
ALOHA STATE

DEALER (KAUAI)

HAWAII — MO-YR
BWS 12
ALOHA STATE

BOARD OF WATER SUPPLY
(HONOLULU ONLY)

FLEET HAWAII — MO-YR
P 12345
ALOHA STATE

FLEET VEHICLE

The "Aloha State" issues two fully-reflectorized license plates. a county code is used in the numbering system. The earlier 1981 base plates with the head of King Kamehameha are being replaced with a new rainbow design; scheduled to be complete by 1994.

Distinctive captions:
ALOHA STATE - Aloha is Hawaiian word of greeting.
FLEET - Used by companies that operate fleets of vehicles.
HORSELESS CARRIAGE - Vehicle 35 years or older.

Codes:
Hawaii is replacing all the older "Hawaiian warrior" graphic plates with a new rainbow design base plate.

Passenger vehicles are 3 alpha - 3 numeric.

The following alpha prefixes indicate county of origin:

AAA - BZZ City and county of Honolulu (Oahu)
HAA -HZZ Hawaii (Island of Hawaii)
MAA - MZZ County of Maui (Maui, Molokai, Lanai)
KAA - KZZ County of Kauai (Island of Kauai)

The following prefixes are reserved for officials:

BUS - Honolulu municipal bus
BWS - Board of Water Supply
C&C - City and County Honolulu
C of H - County of Hawaii
C of K- County of Kauai
C of M - County of Maui

CJ - Chief Justice St. Supreme Court
HFD - Both Hawaii and Honolulu Fire
HPD - Honolulu Police Dept
KFD - Kauai Fire Dept
MFD - Maui Fire Dept

Truck and trailer plates are the same design as passenger plates.
The characters are reversed 3 numeric - 3 alpha.
The first alpha on truck and trailer plates is a county code:

H	County of Hawaii
M	County of Maui
K	County of Kauai
T	City & County of Honolulu truck
W	City & County of Honolulu trailer

Personalized plates application is available from Director of Finance, C & C Honolulu, 1455 S. Beretania St, Honolulu 96814. A maximum of 6 alpha numeric characters (including dash). Fee $25 per year.

To trace the owner of a vehicle contact the Director of Finance in the county.
Oahu - 1455 South Beretania, Honolulu 96814
Hawaii - 25 Aupuni St., Hilo, 96720
Maui - Treasury Division, Wailuku, Maui 96793
Kauai - Division of Treasury, Lihue, 96766
Send the plate number and request an abstract of the registration.

IDAHO

2 PLATES VALIDATED
BY 1 DECAL
ON BOTH PLATES

STATE
ROUTE MARKER

24
IDAHO

COEUR D'ALENE
MOSCOW
BOISE
TWIN FALLS

KBOI 670 Boise
KVNI 1080 Coeur D'Alene
KTFI 1270 Twins Falls
KRPL 1400 Moscow

AM RADIO

CENTENNIAL PLATE
NO COUNTY CODE

PASSENGER
PHASED OUT DURING 1992

PERSONALIZED

PERSONALIZED
(USED UNTIL END OF 92)

HANDICAPPED

DISABLED VETERAN

STATE OWNED

LEGISLATIVE

REPOSSESSION

TRUCK COMMERCIAL

TRUCK LIMITED

PURPLE HEART
RECIPIENT

CONGRESSIONAL
MEDAL OF HONOR
RECIPIENT

PRISONER OF WAR

OLD TIMER

The "Gem State" home of "Famous Potatoes" issues two fully-reflectorized license plates with a unique county code system. Counties are coded alphabetically so the tenth county starting with "B" receives a 10 B prefix.

Distinctive captions:
CLASSIC- Vehicle over 30 years old used for exhibition . The authentic plate program permits an original plate the same year of manufacture to be used on vehicles at least 30 yrs old.
LOANER- Used on dealer vehicles loaned to customers.
STREET ROD- Modified vehicle manufactured prior to 1949.

Codes:

Passenger vehicles, light trucks and trailers are issued plates with an alpha/numeric prefix which indicates the county of origin.
The county (county seat) codes are as follows:

1A	Ada (Boise)	4C	Cassia (Burley)	1M	Madison (Rexburg)
2A	Adams (Council)	5C	Clark (Dubois)	2M	Minidoka (Rupert)
1B	Bannock (Pocatello)	6C	Clearwater (Orofino)	N	Nez Perce
2B	Bear Lake (Paris)	7C	Custer (Challis)		(Lewiston)
3B	Benewah	E	Elmore (Mtn. Home)	10	Oneida (Malad City)
	(St Maries)	1F	Franklin (Preston)	20	Owyhee (Murphy)
4B	Bingham (Blackfoot)	2F	Fremont	1P	Payette (Payette)
5B	Blaine (Hailey)		(St. Anthony)	2P	Power
6B	Boise (Idaho City)	1G	Gem (Emmett)		(American Falls)
7B	Bonner (Sandpoint)	2G	Gooding (Gooding)	S	Shoshone (Wallace)
8B	Bonneville	I	Idaho (Grangeville)	1T	Teton (Driggs)
	(Idaho Falls)	1J	Jefferson (Rigby)	2T	Twin Falls
9B	Boundary	2J	Jerome (Jerome)		(Twin Falls)
	(Bonners Ferry)	K	Kootenai	V	Valley (Cascade)
10B	Butte (Arco)		(Coeur d'Alene)	W	Washington
1C	Camas (Fairfield)	1L	Latah (Moscow)		(Weiser)
2C	Canyon (Caldwell)	2L	Lemhi (Salmon)		
3C	Caribou	3L	Lewis (Nez perce)		
	(Soda Springs)	4L	Lincoln (Shoshone)		

The following alpha prefixes (suffixes) are reserved for special use:

ANG	Air National Guard	**ISP**	Idaho St. Police	**RPO**	Repossession
DL	Dealer	**LAA-LA**	Loaner	(suffix)	TK Truck
DV	Disabled Veteran	**NG**	National Guard	(suffix)	TR Trailer

Idaho does not designate the weight of a vehicle on the plate.
Letters I,O,Q are not used as alpha characters on Idaho plates

Personalized plates are available from Motor Vehicle Div. P.O.Box 7129 Boise 83731. 6 alpha / numerics allowed. Plate fee of $6 and $15 annual renewal in addition to regular fees.

To trace the owner of an Idaho registered vehicle contact Motor Veh. Div. P.O.Box 34 Boise 83731. The fee is $4.00 per record requested.

ILLINOIS

STATE ROUTE MARKER

ILLINOIS 99

CHICAGO

SPRINGFIELD

★WMAQ 670 Chicago
★WGN 720 Chicago
★WBBM 780 Chicago
★WLS 890 Chicago
★WLUP 1000 Chicago

AM RADIO

Illinois Land of Lincoln
1 2 3 4 5 6
MO/YR

2 PLATES VALIDATED BY
ONE DECAL AFFIXED
TO THE LOWER CENTER
OF REAR PLATE

Illinois Land of Lincoln
ILL 1 2 3
MO/YR

PASSENGER

Illinois Land of Lincoln
AB 1234
MO/YR

PASSENGER
2 ALPHA - 4 NUMERIC

Illinois Land of Lincoln
ABC 123
MO/YR

PASSENGER
3 ALPHA - 3 NUMERIC

Illinois Land of Lincoln
FOWLER
MO/YR

PERSONALIZED

91 ILLINOIS 92
OFFICIAL **123** HOUSE
LAND OF LINCOLN

ELECTED STATE OFFICIAL
ILLINOIS LEGISLATURE

P LAND OF LINCOLN
U 12345
ILLINOIS

STATE VEHICLE
(SMALL"P" MEANS
PERMANENT PLATE)

Illinois Land of Lincoln
1234 BA B TRUCK
MO/YR

TRUCK 8,000LBS OR LESS
MULTI-YEAR PLATE

JUN ILLINOIS 92
12 345 F
LAND OF LINCOLN

TRUCK
12,001 - 16,000 LBS

JUN ILLINOIS 92
000 T MK
LAND OF LINCOLN

TRUCK TRACTOR
28,001 - 32,000LBS.
MAX. MILES PERMITTED - 7000

Illinois Land of Lincoln
DISABLED VETERAN **V 0000**
MO/YR

DISABLED VETERAN

Illinois Land of Lincoln
ARMED FORCES RESERVES **R 0000**
MO/YR

MILITARY RESERVE

Illinois Land of Lincoln
NATIONAL GUARD **N 0000**
MO/YR

NATIONAL GUARD

Illinois Land of Lincoln
PURPLE HEART **A 0000**
MO/YR

PURPLE HEART
RECIPIENT

Illinois Land of Lincoln
GOLD STAR **G 0000**
MO/YR

THOSE AWARDED
THE GOLD STAR

Illinois Land of Lincoln
CONGRESSIONAL MEDAL OF HONOR **ABC CMH**
MO/YR

CONGRESSIONAL
MEDAL OF HONOR
RECIPIENT
INITIALS FIRST 3 ALPHAS

36

The "Land of Lincoln" issues two fully-reflectorized license plates. Illinois which produces more varieties of plates than any other state, issues a large number of annual (fiscal year) plates for non passenger vehicles.

Distinctive captions:

CEREMONIAL: A parade vehicle.
LIVERY- A rent-a car and passenger vehicle for hire.
REPOSSESSOR: Used to repossess motor vehicles.

Codes:

Passenger plates are issued for the calendar year.and are:
all numeric; 2 alpha-4 numeric,   3 alpha-3 numeric, 3 alpha- 4 numeric

Prefixes reserved for special groups and vehicle classifications:

DAV	- Disabled Veteran	**MFR**	-Vehicle manufacturer
D over **L**	- Dealer	**P** over **R**	-Prorated vehicle
F over **H**	- Funeral home	**U**	-State owned vehicle
I over **T**	- Transporter plate	**CV** (suffix)	- Non profit org.
M	- County, town, mun.		

Trucks and other commercial vehicles operating intrastate (only within Illinois) receive plates by the fiscal year July - June. Trucks operating interstate are issued prorated or apportioned plates on a calendar basis Jan. - Dec. The numeric characters on these plates are solely for individual vehicle identification. The last (or bottom) alpha character is a weight code:

Suffix	Gross weight (lbs)	Suffix	Gross weight (lbs)
B	8,000 lbs or less	V	64,001 - 73,280
D	8,001 -12,000	X	73,281 - 77,000
F	12,001 - 16,000	Z	77,001 - 80,000
H	16,001 - 24,000	T over A (trailer)	3,000 or less
J	24,001 -28,000	B	3,001 - 8000
K	28,001 - 32,000	C	8,001 - 10,000
N	32,000 - 41,000	E	10,001 - 14,000
P	41,001 - 45,000	G	14,001 - 20,000
R	45,001 - 50,000	K	20,001 - 32,000
S	50,001 - 59,500	L	32,001 - 36,000
T	51,001 - 64,000	N	36,001 - 40,000
T	59,501 - 64,000		

Other codes found in alpha suffixes

BM - Municipal bus	**FM** - Farm machinery	**S** over **T**- Semi trailer
CB - Charitable org.	**M** - Mileage tax plate	**T** over second alpha- full trailer
CN - Conservation plate	**PM** - Permanent equip.	
F over **T** - Farm trailer	**P** over **R** - Prorated	

Personalized plates are available through Office of Secretary of State, Special plate section, Springfield 62756. Maximum of 7 characters. Fee $48 for cars. Vanity plates 6 letters or just 1,2,3 numerics is $75 initial charge.

To trace the owner of an Illinois registered vehicle, write the Secretary of State's office in Springfield. Send $2.00 for each record requested.

INDIANA

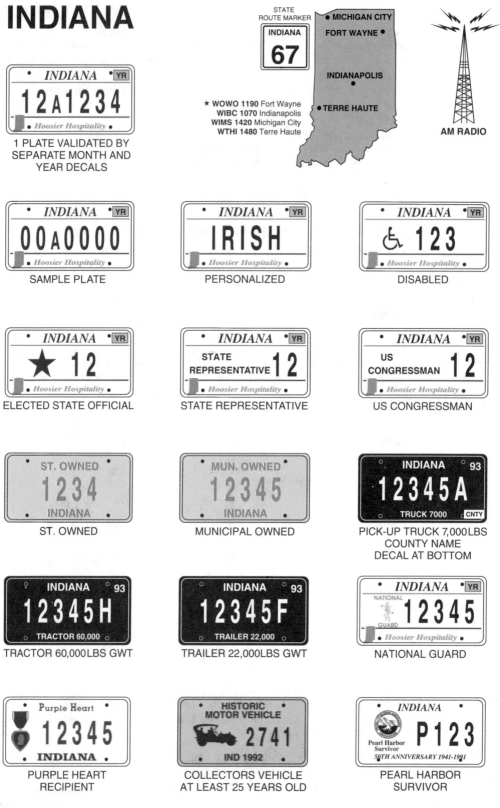

STATE ROUTE MARKER

INDIANA
67

● MICHIGAN CITY
FORT WAYNE ●

INDIANAPOLIS
●

● TERRE HAUTE

★ WOWO 1190 Fort Wayne
WIBC 1070 Indianapolis
WIMS 1420 Michigan City
WTHI 1480 Terre Haute

AM RADIO

INDIANA · YR
12A1234
· Hoosier Hospitality ·

1 PLATE VALIDATED BY
SEPARATE MONTH AND
YEAR DECALS

INDIANA · YR
00A0000
· Hoosier Hospitality ·

SAMPLE PLATE

INDIANA · YR
IRISH
· Hoosier Hospitality ·

PERSONALIZED

INDIANA · YR
♿ **123**
· Hoosier Hospitality ·

DISABLED

INDIANA · YR
★ **12**
· Hoosier Hospitality ·

ELECTED STATE OFFICIAL

INDIANA · YR
STATE
REPRESENTATIVE **12**
· Hoosier Hospitality ·

STATE REPRESENTATIVE

INDIANA · YR
US
CONGRESSMAN **12**
· Hoosier Hospitality ·

US CONGRESSMAN

ST. OWNED
1234
INDIANA

ST. OWNED

MUN. OWNED
12345
INDIANA

MUNICIPAL OWNED

INDIANA 93
12345A
TRUCK 7000 CNTY

PICK-UP TRUCK 7,000LBS
COUNTY NAME
DECAL AT BOTTOM

INDIANA 93
12345H
TRACTOR 60,000

TRACTOR 60,000LBS GWT

INDIANA 93
12345F
TRAILER 22,000

TRAILER 22,000LBS GWT

INDIANA · YR
NATIONAL
GUARD **12345**
· Hoosier Hospitality ·

NATIONAL GUARD

Purple Heart
12345
INDIANA

PURPLE HEART
RECIPIENT

HISTORIC
MOTOR VEHICLE
2741
IND 1992

COLLECTORS VEHICLE
AT LEAST 25 YEARS OLD

INDIANA
Pearl Harbor
Survivor
50TH ANNIVERSARY 1941-1991
P123

PEARL HARBOR
SURVIVOR

"The "Home of Hoosier Hospitality" issues one fully-reflectorized license plate. A county code system is used in the numeric prefix. A small county decal also appears on the plate.

Distinctive captions:
HOUSE CAR - Vehicle one can live in, SCHOOL T.C. - Driver training car
Codes:
Private passenger vehicles and light truck plates (pickups) have a numeric prefix that is a county code. A small county name decal also appears in the lower right corner of each passenger and light truck plate. The 1 alpha and 4 numeric characters that follow have no special significance other than identify the individual vehicle. The county and (County seats) are as follows:

1. **Adams** (Decatur)	26. **Gibson** (Princeton)	51. **Martin** (Shoals)	76. **Steuben** (Angola)
2. **Allen** (Ft. Wayne)	27. **Grant** (Marion)	52. **Miami** (Peru)	77.**Sullivan** (Sullivan)
3. **Bartholomew** (Columbus)	28. **Green** (Bloomfield)	53. **Monroe** (Bloomngtn.)	78. **Switzerland** (Vevay)
4. **Benton** (Fowler)	29. **Hamilton** (Nobles--ville)	54. **Montgomery** (Crawfordsville)	79.**Tippecanoe**(Lafayette)
5. **Blackford** (Hrtfrd Cty.)	30. **Hancock** (Greenfld.)	55. **Morgan** (Martinsville)	80. **Tipton** (Tipton)
6. **Boone** (Lebanon)	31. **Harrison** (Corydon)	56. **Newton** (Kentland)	81. **Union** (Liberty)
7. **Brown** (Nashville)	32. **Hendricks** (Dansville)	57. **Noble** (Albion)	82. **Vanderburgh** (Evansville)
8. **Carrol** (Delphi)	33. **Henry** (New Castle)	58. **Ohio** (Rising Sun)	83. **Vermillion** (Newport)
9. **Cass** (Loganport)	34. **Howard** (Kokomo)	59. **Orange** (Paoli)	84.**Vigo** (Terre Haute)
10. **Clark** (Jeffersonville)	35. **Huntington** (Hntgtn.)	60. **Owen** (Spencer)	85. **Wabash** (Wabash)
11. **Clay** (Brazil)	36.**Jackson** (Brwnstwn.)	61. **Parke** (Rockville)	86. **Warren**(Williamsport)
12. **Clinton** (Frankfort)	37. **Jasper** (Rnsselaer.)	62. **Perry** (Cannelton)	87. **Warrick** (Bonneville)
13. **Crawford** (English)	38 **Jay** (Portland)	63. **Pike** (Petersburg)	88. **Washington** (Salem)
14. **Daviess**(Washngtn.)	39. **Jefferson** (Madison)	64. **Porter** (Valpariso)	89. **Wayne** (Richmond)
15. **Dearborn** (Lwrncbrg)	40. **Jennings** (Vernon)	65. **Posey** (Mt Vernon)	90. **Wells** (Bluffton)
16. **Decatur** (Grensbrg.)	41. **Johnson** (Franklin)	66. **Pulaski** (Winamac)	91. **White** (Montecello)
17. **DeKalb** (Auburn)	42. **Knox** (Vincennes)	67. **Putnam**(Greencstle.)	92. **Whitley**(Colmb. Cty.)
18. **Delaware** (Muncie)	43.**Kosciusko** (Warsaw)	68. **Randolph**(Winchstr.)	93. **Marion** (Indianapolis)
19. **Dubois** (Jasper)	44.**Lagrange**(Lagrange)	69. **Ripley** (Versailles)	94. **Lake** (Crown Point)
20. **Elkhart** Goshen)	45. **Lake** (Crown Point)	70. **Rush** (Rushville)	95A. **Military& Special**
21. **Fayette**(Connersville)	46. **La Porte** (La Porte)	71. **St.Joseph**(S. Bend)	95B -Z. **Marion** (Indianapolis)
22. **Floyd** (New Albany)	47. **Lawrence** (Bedford)	72. **Scott** (Scottsburg)	96 **Lake** (Crown Point)
23. **Fountain** (Covington)	48. **Madison** (Anderson)	73. **Shelby** (Shelbyville)	97-99 **Marion** (Indianapolis)
24. **Franklin** (Brookville)	49. **Marion** (Indianapolis)	74. **Spencer** (Rockport)	
25. **Fulton** (Rochester)	50. **Marshall** (Plymouth)	75. **Starke** (Knox)	

Elected and appointed state officials have special plates captioned with a star. Low numbers are reserved for the following:

1. - Governor	5.- Treasurer	9-Clerk Supreme & Appellate Ct
2. - Lt. Governor	6.- Attorney. General	10-14 - Supreme Court Justices
3. - Secretary. of State	7. - Supt. of Schools	15 - 27 -Appellate Court Judges
4. - Auditor	8.- Recorder Supreme & Appellate	

Truck, truck tractor and trailer plates are issued new every February. Instead of a county code, they have a small numeric at the top of the plate that shows the weight class i.e. (26) indicates 26 to 36,000lbs gross vehicle wgt class.

Bus plate prefixes mean: A - for hire ; C - Not for hire including non profit org. D- Restricted area, city use bus

Personalized plates are available from registrant's county license bureau. 7 characters and a space will be considered, The cost is $40 per year in addition to the regular registration fee.
To trace the owner write to : Paid mail section, Bureau of Motor Vehicles, Rm.416, State Office Bldg, Indianapolis IN 46204. Include plate number and request an abstract of the registration. Fee $4.00 per request. For samples contact Special Sales.

IOWA

STATE ROUTE MARKER
17

★ **WHO 1040** Des Moines
WMT 600 Cedar Falls
WOC 1420 Davenport
KGLO 1300 Mason City

MASON CITY
CEDAR FALLS
DES MOINES
DAVENPORT

AM RADIO

IOWA 86
ABC 123
MO DUBUQUE YR

2 PLATES VALIDATED BY
2 DECALS
ON REAR PLATE

SESQUICENTENNIAL 1846 ◊ 1996 **IOWA**
TC 789

SESQUICENTENNIAL
1846-1996

1846 - 1996 **IOWA** 92
KIRSTEN
MO Sesquicentennial YR

SESQUICENTENNIAL
PERSONALIZED
2-7 CHARACTERS

IOWA 81
E 783
MO YR

HANDICAPPED

IOWA
10027
OFFICIAL STATE

STATE OWNED VEHICLE

IOWA
25503
OFFICIAL COUNTY

COUNTY OWNED VEHICLE

IOWA
93703
OFFICIAL

TAX EXEMPT VEHICLE
NOT GOVERNMENT
(RED CROSS, FIRE DEPT., ETC.)

IOWA
★**282**★
STATE PATROL

STATE POLICE

IOWA 86
ER 9140
MO POLK YR

TRUCK

IOWA 86
SP 1235
MO SPECIAL YR

PRIVATE FARM TRUCK
NOT FOR HIRE
RESTRICTED USE

IOWA UNI 89
UNI0432
PANTHERS

NORTHERN IOWA
PANTHERS

IOWA ISU 89
ISU1856
CYCLONES

IOWA STATE UNIVERSITY
CYCLONES

IOWA 89
UI 1682
HAWKEYES

UNIVERSITY OF IOWA
HAWKEYES

IOWA 91
P114
YR

PEARL HARBOR
SURVIVOR

IOWA 90
01093
MO Combat Wounded YR

PURPLE HEART
RECIPIENT

IOWA
1CMH
MO YR

CONGRESSIONAL
MEDAL OF HONOR
RECIPIENT

The "Hawkeye State" issues two partially-reflectorized (glass beads on paint) license plates. Many recent specialized plates are made of reflectorized sheeting. The county name is embossed on the bottom of most plates.

Distinctive captions:

SME: Special mobile equipment (construction equipment)
RESTRICTED: Nonstandard vehicle limited highway use.
ANTIQUE: Motor vehicle at least 25 years old for limited use on highway.
OFFICIAL SCHOOL: Owned by Iowa Independent School District

Codes:

Passenger vehicle plates display 3 alpha - 3 numeric characters. The county name appears on the lower center of the plate.

Trucks and commercial vehicle plates have the same design as passenger, however the characters are 2 alpha- 4 numeric. The following alpha characters are reserved for special use:

LAA - ZZZ - Passenger cars
AA - JZ - Truck, full year
B - J - Handicapped
D - Dealer
KA - KZ - Truck, tractor full yr
IAA - IZZ - Antique vehicle
DAA - EZZ - Semitrailer
JAA - JZZ - Travel trailer
LD - Urban transit bus
SA - SZ - Special truck full yr

DV - Disabled veteran
LF - LZ - Special mobile equipment
PA - Apportioned truck full yr.
RA - Apportioned trailer.
RL - Apportioned trailer, semi trailer 3 yrs.
XX - Restricted vehicle
X - National guard
Z- Special plate issued to third time DUI offender - permits law enforcement to stop and inspect the vehicle at any time.

Personalized plate applications are available through the office of the county treasurer Drivers License Stations, and the Dept of Transportation, office of Vehicle Registration, Park Fair Mall, 100 Euclid Ave. P.O.Box 9204 Des Moines IA 50306. Fee is $25 for original application, $5 when plates are validated each year, and $25 when new plates are issued. 2 - 7 characters are permitted.

To trace the owner of an Iowa registered vehicle, vehicle registration records are open for public inspection during business hours. Records search fee is $2.70 per 15 minutes or fraction thereof. Requests must be directed to : Dept of Transportation, Office of Vehicle Registration, 100 Euclid Ave, Des Moines IA 50306-9204

KANSAS

STATE ROUTE MARKER

5

KFKU 1250 Lawrence
KKSU 580 Manhattan
KFRM 550 Salina

MANHATTAN
LAWRENCE
SALINA

AM RADIO

SN KANSAS 89
EBC 123
1 PLATE VALIDATED BY
3 DECALS (MO/YR/COUNTY)

SN KANSAS 89
ABC 211
PASSENGER REGULAR
1989 ISSUE

LY KANSAS YR/MO
WHEAT
PERSONALIZED
2 PLATES ISSUED

KANSAS 89
♿ 123
DISABLED

KANSAS 89
DCO 123
DISABLED PERSON
DRIVER TRAINING

KANSAS
1234
OFFICIAL
STATE OWNED VEHICLE

KANSAS
101
HIGHWAY PATROL
HIGHWAY PATROL

SN KANSAS 89
ABC 123
12M REGULAR
TRUCK

SN KANSAS 89
ABC 123
20M
TRAILER

KANSAS 91
TRUCK 16000
APPORTIONED
INTERSTATE TRUCK
APPORTIONED

KANSAS 89
SPEC 1234 VEH
STREET ROD
COLLECTOR'S VEHICLE
MANUFACTURED BEFORE 1949

KANSAS
9 2 1234
KCC
KANSAS COMMODITY
COMMISSION
COLOR CHANGES YEARLY

KANSAS
KCC 1234 TAG
EQUIPMENT
OIL WELL EQUIPMENT
& PULLING UNITS

KANSAS 89
WØABC
AMATEUR RADIO

KANSAS
1234
NATIONAL GUARD
NATIONAL GUARD

KANSAS
1234
EX-PRISONER OF WAR
EX-PRISONER OF WAR

The "Sunflower State" issues one fully-reflectorized license plate, each containing a small two-letter county designation decal in the upper left corner of the plate. Personalized plates are issued in pairs. The state name has been made easier to read on recent issues.

Distinctive captions:

DRIVE AWAY: Drive away operator other than dealer.

FULL USE: Dealer plate that can be used on any vehicle.

KCC: Kansas Corporation Commission plate issued to private carriers of commodities.

Codes:

Kansas uses a 2 alpha county code on passenger plates. It appears on a sticker on the upper left corner of the plate. The counties and (County seats) are as follows:

AL ALLEN (Iola)	**GL** GREELEY (Tribune)	**OB** OSBORNE (Osborne)
AN ANDERSON (Garnett)	**GW** GREENWOOD (Eureka)	**OT** OTTAWA(Minneapolis)
AT ATCHISON (Atchison)	**HM** HAMILTON (Syracuse)	**PN** PAWNEE (Larned)
AB BARBER (Medicine lodge)	**HP** HARPER (Anthony)	**PL** PHILLIPS (Phillipsburg)
BT BARTON (Great Bend)	**HV** HARVEY (Newton)	**PT** POTTAWATOMIE (Westmoreland)
BB BOURBON (Ft. Scott)	**HS** HASKELL (Sublette)	**PR** PRATT (Pratt)
BR BROWN (Hiawatha)	**HG** HODGEMAN (Jetmore)	**RA** RAWLINS (Atwood)
BU BUTLER (El Dorado)	**JA** JACKSON (Holton)	**RN** RENO (Hutchinson)
CS CHASE (Ctnwood Falls)	**JF** JEFFERSON(Oskaloosa)	**RP** REPUBLIC (Belleville)
CQ CHAUTAUQUA (Sedan)	**JW** JEWELL (Mankato)	**RC** RICE (Lyons)
CK CHEROKEE (Columbus)	**JO** JOHNSON (Olathe)	**RL** RILEY (Manhattan)
CN CHEYENNE (St Francis)	**KE** KEARNEY (Lakin)	**RO** ROOKS (Stockton)
CA CLARK (Ashland)	**KM** KINGMAN (Kingman)	**RH** RUSH (La Crosse)
CY CLAY (Clay Center)	**KW** KIOWA (Greensburg)	**RS** RUSSELL (Russell)
CD CLOUD (Concordia)	**LB** LABETTE (Oswego)	**SA** SALINE (Salina)
CF COFFEE (Burlington)	**LE** LANE (Dighton)	**SC** SCOTT (Scott City)
CM COMANCHE (Coldwtr.)	**LV** LEAVENWORTH (Leavenworth)	**SG** SEDGWICK (Wichita)
CL COWLEY (Winfield)	**LC** LINCOLN (Lincoln)	**SW** SEWARD (Liberal)
CR CRAWFORD (Girard)	**LN** LINN (Mound City)	**SN** SHAWNEE (Topeka)
DC DECATUR (Oberlin)	**LG** LOGAN (Oakley)	**SD** SHERIDAN (Hoxie)
DK DICKINSON Abilene)	**LY** LYON (Emporia)	**SH** SHERMAN (Goodland)
DP DONIPHAN (Troy)	**MN** MARION (Marion)	**SM** SMITH (Smith Center)
DG DOUGLAS (Lawrence)	**MS** MARSHALL (Marysville)	**SF** STAFFORD (St John)
ED EDWARDS (Kinsley)	**MP** McPHERSON (McPherson)	**ST** STANTON (Johnson)
EK ELK (Howard)	**ME** MEADE (Meade)	**SV** STEVENS (Hugoton)
EL ELLIS (Hays)	**MI** MIAMI (Paola)	**SU** SUMNER (Wellington)
EW ELLSWORTH (Ellswrth)	**MC** MITCHELL (Beloit)	**TH** THOMAS (Colby)
FI FINNEY (Garden City)	**MG** MONTGOMERY (Independence)	**TR** TREGO (Wakeeney)
FO FORD (Dodge City)	**MR** MORRIS (Council Grove)	**WB** WABAUNSEE (Alma)
FR FRANKLIN (Ottawa)	**MT** MORTON (Elkhart)	**WA** WALLACE (Sharon Sp.)
GE GEARY (Junction City)	**NM** NEMAHA (Seneca)	**WS** WASHINGTON (Wash.)
CO GOVE (Gove)	**NO** NEOSHO (Erie)	**WH** WICHITA (Leoti)
GH GRAHAM (Hill City)	**NS** NESS (Ness City)	**WL** WILSON (Fredonia)
GT GRANT (Ulysses)	**NT** NORTON (Norton)	**WO** WOODSON (Yates Ctr.)
GY GRAY (Cimarron)	**OS** OSAGE (Lyndon)	**WY** WYANDOTTE (Kansas City)

The weight class of trucks and trailers is indicated by a decal on the plate.

Personalized plates are available from county treasurers office.1- 7 alpha numeric characters allowed. Fee $40 in addition to regular fee.

Tracing information is available by mail only.Write to Titles and Registration, Dept. of Revenue,State Office Bldg.Topeka 66626. $2.00 fee.

KENTUCKY

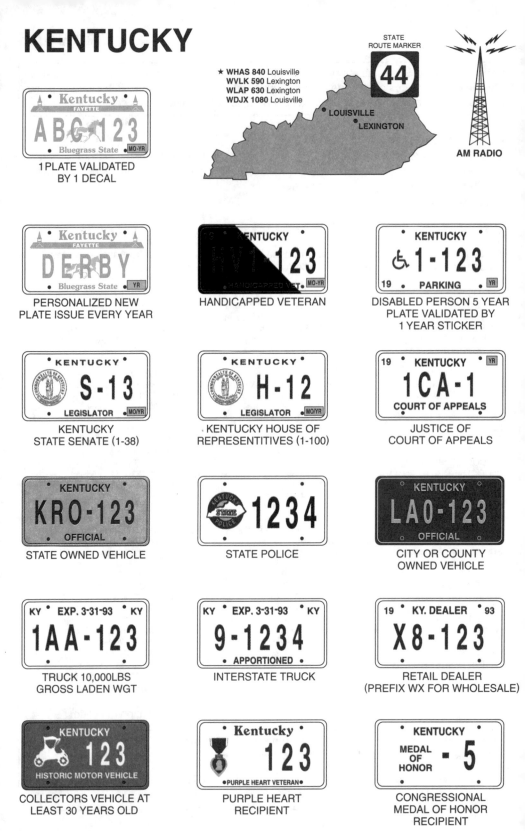

STATE ROUTE MARKER

44

★ WHAS 840 Louisville
WVLK 590 Lexington
WLAP 630 Lexington
WDJX 1080 Louisville

LOUISVILLE
LEXINGTON

AM RADIO

Kentucky
FAYETTE
A B G · 1 2 3
Bluegrass State · MO-YR
1 PLATE VALIDATED
BY 1 DECAL

Kentucky
FAYETTE
D E R B Y
Bluegrass State · YR
PERSONALIZED NEW
PLATE ISSUE EVERY YEAR

KENTUCKY
HV · 1 2 3
HANDICAPPED VET · MO-YR
HANDICAPPED VETERAN

KENTUCKY
♿ 1 - 1 2 3
19 · PARKING · YR
DISABLED PERSON 5 YEAR
PLATE VALIDATED BY
1 YEAR STICKER

KENTUCKY
S - 1 3
LEGISLATOR · MO/YR
KENTUCKY
STATE SENATE (1-38)

KENTUCKY
H - 1 2
LEGISLATOR · MO/YR
KENTUCKY HOUSE OF
REPRESENTITIVES (1-100)

19 · KENTUCKY · YR
1 C A - 1
COURT OF APPEALS
JUSTICE OF
COURT OF APPEALS

KENTUCKY
K R O · 1 2 3
OFFICIAL
STATE OWNED VEHICLE

KENTUCKY
1 2 3 4
STATE POLICE

KENTUCKY
L A 0 - 1 2 3
OFFICIAL
CITY OR COUNTY
OWNED VEHICLE

KY · EXP. 3-31-93 · KY
1 A A - 1 2 3
TRUCK 10,000LBS
GROSS LADEN WGT

KY · EXP. 3-31-93 · KY
9 - 1 2 3 4
· APPORTIONED ·
INTERSTATE TRUCK

19 · KY. DEALER · 93
X 8 - 1 2 3
RETAIL DEALER
(PREFIX WX FOR WHOLESALE)

KENTUCKY
1 2 3
HISTORIC MOTOR VEHICLE
COLLECTORS VEHICLE AT
LEAST 30 YEARS OLD

Kentucky
1 2 3
·PURPLE HEART VETERAN·
PURPLE HEART
RECIPIENT

KENTUCKY
MEDAL
OF - 5
HONOR
CONGRESSIONAL
MEDAL OF HONOR
RECIPIENT

The "Bluegrass State" issues one fully-reflectorized license plate for all passenger vehicles. A county name decal appears under the state name. Kentucky issues many annual non-passenger plates which are not reflectorized.

Distinctive captions:

HISTORIC - Vehicle at least 30 years old
JUDICIARY - Judge in the Kentucky judicial system
LIMITED - Truck that pays a limited registration fee. This includes vehicles hauling forest products, limited area of operations and other exemptions.
PARKING - Special parking privileges.
TRANSPORTATION - Kentucky Dept. of Transportation
TRUCK TRAILER - Semitrailer
By state law, all Kentucky private and commercial license plates are blue and white. The colors are reversed with new issues.

Codes:

Kentucky passenger vehicle plates have 3 alpha- 3 numeric characters and the county name appears at the top of the plate. The alpha numeric combinations are for individual vehicle identification only, there are no codes.

Official state owned vehicle plates usually begin with **K**, and there is no department or use numbering system.

County and city owned vehicles usually begin with **L**. There is no other significance to the alpha numeric numbering system.

Owners of personalized plates receive new plates every year. The design remains the same for a 5 year period, but new plates are issued annually.

Truck plates have 2 alpha and 4 numerics that appear in various positions.

Truck plates do not indicate county of origin. Any special use, weight class and restrictions appear as captions on the plate.

Dealer plates identify wholesale dealers with **WX** and retail dealers **X**.

Apportioned vehicle plates begin with the numeric 9, and do not have either county of origin and weight class indicated.

Personalized plates applications are available through the Dept. of Vehicle Regulation in Frankfort, or County Court Clerk offices throughout the state. The fee is $25 per year, in addition to the regular registration fee. Any alpha numeric combination, up to 6 characters will be considered.

To trace the owner of a Kentucky registered vehicle write to Dept. of Vehicle Licensing, State Office Bldg., Frankfort KY 40622. Request an abstract of the registration. The fee is $3.00 per inquiry. Use this address for sample requests.

LOUISIANA

STATE
ROUTE MARKER

LA 1

SHREVEPORT

BATON ROUGE

NEW ORLEANS

★ WWL 870 New Orleans
★ KWKH 1130 Shreveport
WXOK 1460 Baton Rouge

AM RADIO

SPORTSMAN'S PARADISE
456 A 789
LoUiSiAna MO-YR

1 PLATE VALIDATED
BY 1 MO/YR DECAL

SPORTSMAN'S PARADISE
333 X 123
LOUISIANA MO-YR

PASSENGER OLDER ISSUE
STILL IN USE

- Louisiana -
423 A 456
World's Fair MO-YR

1984 WORLD'S FAIR
PASSENGER OLDER ISSUE
STILL IN USE

- BAYOU STATE -
11 A 111
MO LOUISIANA YR

PASSENGER OLDER ISSUE
STILL IN USE

PERSONALIZED
ALBERT
LOUISIANA MO-YR

PERSONALIZED

HANDICAPPED
00005
LOUISIANA MO-YR

HANDICAPPED

HEARING IMPAIRED
96
LOUISIANA MO-YR

HEARING IMPAIRED
DRIVER

- PRIVATE -
S568122
LOUISIANA MO-YR

PRIVATE TRUCK
UNDER 6000 LBS

PRIVATE TRUCK
B269247
LOUISIANA MO-YR

PRIVATE TRUCK
OVER 6001 LBS

- VOL. FIRE FIGHTER -
F 772
Louisana MO-YR

VOLUNTEER FIREMAN

★ PEARL HARBOR SURVIVOR ★
79
LOUISIANA MO-YR

PEARL HARBOR
SURVIVOR

- LAW OFFICER -
RETIRED **123**
LoUiSiAna MO-YR

RETIRED LAW OFFICER
(CITY POLICE)

- CIVIL AIR PATROL -
31
LOUISIANA MO-YR

CIVIL AIR PATROL

KOREAN WAR
ARMY **14**
LoUiSiAna MO-YR

KOREAN VETERAN

- VIETNAM VETERAN -
NAVY **14**
LOUISIANA

VIETNAM VETERAN

- LOUISIANA -
P H **63**
- PURPLE HEART -

PURPLE HEART
RECIPIENT
PERMANENT PLATE

The "Sportsman's Paradise" issues one fully-reflectorized license plate. Passenger plates are issued by State Police Troop area, with the letter in the center of the plate designating the troop. Louisiana has not had a general plate re-issue since 1974, and currently there are five different bases in use.

Distinctive captions:

ANTIQUE -Vehicle over 25 yrs.
CUT - City use Truck
FP- Forest products truck
FU - Farm Use
PO - Private owner
POS - Private semitrailer

PUBLIC -State & municipal veh.
SHRINER - Parade vehicle
STREET ROD - Modified vehicle made in USA before 1949
XPOW - Former prisoner of war
DV - Disabled veteran
GROTTO - Parade vehicle

Codes:

Passenger plates have 4 - 7 numerics with 1 alpha. The alpha designates the Louisiana State Police troop area in which the plate was issued:

A	Baton Rouge	H	Leesville
B	New Orleans	I	Lafayette
C	Raceland	K	Opelousas
D	Lake Charles	L	Covington
E	Alexandria	N	New Orleans
F	Monroe	X	Baton Rouge &
G	Shreveport		statewide mail

Truck, trailer, commercial and other special vehicles are issued plates with an alpha prefix that indicates the vehicle class or special use.

A - Private bus,school bus, road tractor house trailer, commercial
B - Private truck 6,001- 18,000 lbs.
C - Common carrier truck; tractor
D - Light, boat and semitrailer
E - Trailer
F - Farm vehicle

H - Handicapped person
J - Vehicle transporting forest products
M - City use
P- Apportioned
R, S,T - Private truck up to 6,000 lbs.
Y - Long term trailer

Personalized plate application (form VEH-13S) is available from Dept of Public Safety, Vehicle Registration Bureau, P.O.Box 64886, Baton Rouge 70896. Any alpha numeric combination of up to 7 characters is permitted. Only English letters allowed. Fee for autos is $50 in addition to regular 2 yr. fee, motorcycles and trucks are $100 plus 4 year regular registration fee.

To trace the owner of a Louisiana registered vehicle write to:Vehicle Registration, Dept.of Public Safety , P.O.Box 64886, Baton Rouge 70896-4886 attn. Special processing. Fee is $2.00 for information on each plate number requested, plus a $5.50 handling charge.

MAINE

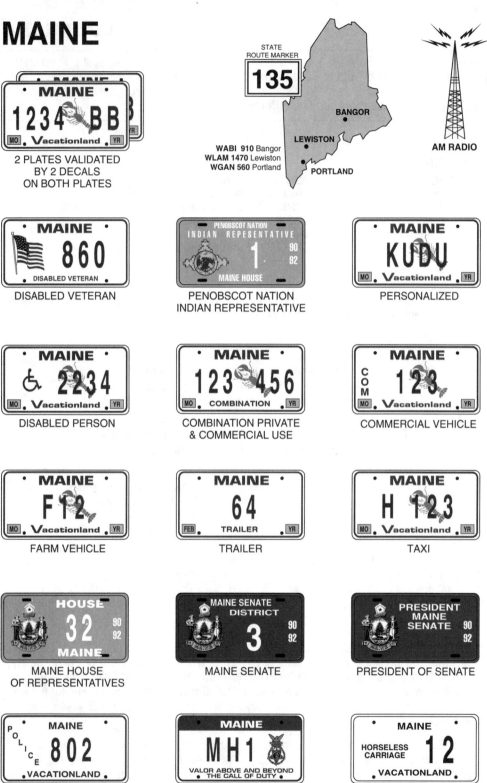

STATE
ROUTE MARKER
135

BANGOR
LEWISTON
PORTLAND

WABI 910 Bangor
WLAM 1470 Lewiston
WGAN 560 Portland

AM RADIO

MAINE 1234 BB
MO · Vacationland · YR
2 PLATES VALIDATED
BY 2 DECALS
ON BOTH PLATES

MAINE 860
DISABLED VETERAN
DISABLED VETERAN

PENOBSCOT NATION
INDIAN REPRESENTATIVE 1 90 92
MAINE HOUSE
PENOBSCOT NATION
INDIAN REPRESENTATIVE

MAINE KUDU
MO · Vacationland · YR
PERSONALIZED

MAINE 2234
MO · Vacationland · YR
DISABLED PERSON

MAINE 123 456
MO · COMBINATION · YR
COMBINATION PRIVATE
& COMMERCIAL USE

MAINE COM 123
MO · Vacationland · YR
COMMERCIAL VEHICLE

MAINE F12
MO · Vacationland · YR
FARM VEHICLE

MAINE 64
FEB · TRAILER · YR
TRAILER

MAINE H 123
MO · Vacationland · YR
TAXI

HOUSE 32 90 92 MAINE
MAINE HOUSE
OF REPRESENTATIVES

MAINE SENATE
DISTRICT 3 90 92
MAINE SENATE

PRESIDENT
MAINE
SENATE 90 92
PRESIDENT OF SENATE

POLICE **MAINE** 802
· VACATIONLAND ·
POLICE

MAINE MH1
VALOR ABOVE AND BEYOND
THE CALL OF DUTY
CONGRESSIONAL
MEDAL OF HONOR
RECIPIENT

MAINE HORSELESS CARRIAGE 12
· VACATIONLAND ·
COLLECTOR'S VEHICLE
1916 AND EARLER

MAINE

America's "Vacationland" issues two fully-reflectorized plates; most have a red lobster graphic background. Until recently Maine passenger plates were all numeric. Currently they are being issued with a two letter suffix.

Distinctive captions:
COACH: Ambulance, funeral coach and hearse.
INDIAN REPRESENTATIVE - Representative of Indian Tribes at the Maine State Legislature.
EQUIPMENT- Towed equipment such as cement mixer etc.
LIVESTOCK AND POULTRY - Issued by Maine Dept of Agriculture to livestock and poultry dealers.

Codes
Passenger vehicle plates have 1 - 6 characters (all numeric or 1 or 2 alpha suffix).
All passenger plates are graphic, with the red lobster in the background. Commercial vehicle plates are all numeric and are clearly captioned. The following prefix codes are used:

COM	All trucks and tractors
D	New car dealers
F	Farm truck
H	Passenger veh. for hire
LT TRAILER	Long term trailer registration
NC, UC	New and Used car dealers

Maine does not issue special occupational plates or designate the county of origin, weight or use restriction on license plates.

Maine license plate numbering system
1-999999
1A-99999A
1B-99999Z
1AA-9999AA
1BB-9999ZZ
1AB-9999AB
AC,AD,etc;BA,BC,BD etc
Lobster base started in "R" suffix
The old '74 base black on white plates came off the road in 1988.

Personalized plates are available for Maine Motor Vehicle Division, Augusta 04333. The initial fee is $15 in addition to the regular registration fee. 1-6 characters can be selected, however no alpha characters may follow the numerics.
To trace the owner of a vehicle through the plate number write to: Motor Vehicle Division, 1 Child St., Augusta, ME 04333. Give the plate number and request a photocopy of the registration. The fee is $2 per record .

MARYLAND

2 PLATES VALIDATED BY 2 DECALS ON REAR PLATE

ABC♦123

STATE ROUTE MARKER

MARYLAND 16

★ **WBAL 1090** Baltimore
WGMS 570 Bethesda
WASA 1330 Harve de Grace

HARVE DE GRACE
BALTIMORE
BETHESDA

AM RADIO

001 AAA
Treasure the Chesapeake
SAVE THE BAY COMMEMORATIVE PLATE

LAURA
PERSONALIZED

&♿ 00001 HC
HANDICAPPED

DV00001
DISABLED VETERAN

SG♦00001
STATE OWNED VEHICLE

LG♦00001
LOCAL GOVERNMENT OWNED VEHICLE

00001 NG
National Guard
NATIONAL GUARD

300♦000
TRUCKS

123♦01 FT
Farm
FARM TRUCK

K3DRN
AMATEUR RADIO

123♦01F
TRUCK TRACTOR

1A00001
Dealer
DEALER

30001
Historic
HISTORIC MOTOR VEHICLE

FD 12345
Firemens Assoc.
FIREMENS ASSOCIATION

BPD0001
Balto Pro Duckpin Assoc.
BALTIMORE PROFESSIONAL DUCKPIN ASSOC.
(SPECIAL PLATE)

The "Old Line State" issues two fully-reflectorized license plates. Passenger and many other non-passenger types display the colorful state shield. A special plate to save the Chesapeake Bay is now available for an additional $20 fee.

Distinctive captions:

FARM AREA: Vehicles permitted to operate on public road adjacent to a farm.
FINANCE: Repossessed vehicle transporter plate.
RECYCLER: Auto wreckers and scrap processors.
TRANS: Transporter

Codes:

Maryland passenger cars are issued 3 alpha-3 numeric plates. The following alpha combinations are reserved for specific classes of vehicles:

Suffix **B** - Taxi, limousine
Suffix **C** - Ambulance, funeral vehicle
DV - Disabled veteran
D over **R**- Daily rental
Suffix **D** - Dump service
Suffix **F** - Truck tractors
F over **T** - Farm truck
H over **C** - Handicapped
I (capital i) - Buses for hire

Suffix **J** - Passenger vans (van pool)
L over **G** - Local government
Suffix **K** - Farm vehicle limited highway use
Suffix **L** - Historic Motor vehicle
Suffix **M** - Multi-purpose trucks, vans
Suffix **PSC** - Buses for hire
S over **G** - State government vehicle
TT - Tow truck

Maryland reserves the following prefixes for special groups: * **no caption appears at the bottom of these plates.**

AG	Ali Ghan Shrine Temple	FOE	Frat.Order of Eagles	PSY	Psychological Assn
AL	American Legion	FF	MD; DC Firefighters	PW	Ex POW
BBO*	Boumi Temple	FOP*	Frat. Order of Police	QUE	Omega Psi Phi Frat.
BJT	Jerusalem Temple No 4	FMA	Prince Hall Gr.Lodge	RI	Rotary International
BNA*	B'nai B'rith	HGA	Hiram Grand Lodge	ROA	Reserve Officers Assn.
BPD	Balt. Pro Duckpin Assc.	HNA	Holy Name Society	RSC	Ranger Social Club
BPW	MD. Prof. bus. women	HPC	Hawks Pleasure Club	RX	Pharmacist Assn
CAP	Civil Air Patrol	JHU	Johns Hopkins Alumni	SKI	Baltimore Ski Club
CCC*	Grace Bible Church	JWV	Jewish War Veterans	TCL	Tall Cedars
CDA	Cath. Dau. of America	KAP	Kappa Alpha Psi	TJA	Trial Judges Assn
CGA	Coast Guard Auxiliary	KC	Knights of Columbus	TPA	Telephone Pioneers
CGR	Coast Guard Reserve	KOP	Knights of Pythias	TSU	Towson State Alumni
CMH	Medal of Honor	LCO	Lions Club International	UAW	Unit. Auto Workers 239
DAV	Disabled Amer.veteran	MP	Maryland Press Club	UM	Univ. of Maryland Alum.
DCC	St. Dem. Cntrl Comm.	Suffix NG	National Guard	VFW	Vet. of Foreign Wars
DDS	Dr. of Dental Surgery	ND	Notre Dame Club	VB	Vulcan Blazers
EAA	Exper. Aircraft Assn.	OPT	Optimist Club	YG*	Yedz Grotto
EEE	Free State Square Club	OSI	Sons of Italy		
ELK	Elks Club	PSU	Penn State Alumni		

Maryland does not designate either county or weight of a vehicle on the plate.

Personalized plates are available from Motor Vehicle Administration, 6601 Richie Highway NE, Glen Burnie, 21060. Permitted combinations: 2 -7 alpha and numeric, all alpha 2 -7, all numeric 5-7 characters, Fee $25 per yr. plus normal registration fee.

To trace the owner of a Maryland plate- registration records are public record and available on video terminal at Motor Vehicle Administration in Glen Burnie. Request by mail cost $2.00 per record for a certified copy.

MASSACHUSETTS

STATE ROUTE MARKER

99

PITTSFIELD

BOSTON

SPRINGFIELD

★ **WBZ 1030** Boston
WHDH 850 Boston
WRKO 680 Boston
WUHN 1110 Pittsfield
WNNZ 640 Springfield

AM RADIO

MASSACHUSETTS MO/YR
123·456

2 PLATES VALIDATED
BY 1 DECAL ON
BOTH PLATES

APR *Massachusetts* YR
1234
● The Spirit of America ●

RESERVED SERIES
5 CHARACTERS OR LESS
ALL NUMERIC OR 1 ALPHA

Massachusetts NOV/YR
PA1952
● The Spirit of America ●

PERSONALIZED
2 PLATES

Massachusetts NOV/YR
1234
Veteran

A PERSON WHO SERVED
DURING WAR TIME

MASSACHUSETTS
M 7111
OFFICIAL

MUNICIPAL

MASSACHUSETTS
POLICE 1482
OFFICIAL

MUNICIPAL POLICE

Massachusetts
123
Official

REGISTRY OF
MOTOR VEHICLES

Massachusetts MO/YR
103-193
● COMMERCIAL ●

TRUCK

Massachusetts MO/YR
102-344
● TRAILER ●

TRAILER

S E N A T E *Massachusetts*
12
● The Spirit of America ●

STATE SENATE

H O U S E *Massachusetts* MO/YR
12
● The Spirit of America ●

MASS. HOUSE OF
REPRESENTATIVES

Massachusetts
EX POW **123**
● The Spirit of America ●

EX POW

Massachusetts MO/YR
K1 DRN
● The Spirit of America ●

AMATEUR RADIO

Massachusetts MO/YR
133
● BIRTHPLACE OF BASKETBALL ●

BASKETBALL HALL OF FAME
AVAILABLE FOR $25 EXTRA FEE

Massachusetts MO/YR
USA 0○○○○○
● The Spirit of America ●

MEMBER OF ANY
OLYMPIC TEAM

OCT *Massachusetts* YR
PURPLE HEART
100
Veteran

PURPLE HEART RECIPIENT

52

MASSACHUSETTS

The "Bay State" issues one fully-reflectorized license plate. Passenger plates are either all numeric or three numeric- three alpha and are green on white. Many of the other plates are issued on the newer red white and blue "The Spirit of America" base plate.

Distinctive captions:
ANTIQUE: A vehicle at least 25 years old.
BOATS: Boat dealer
CAMPER: Autohome
HOUSE: Massachusetts House of Representatives member
NEWS PHOTOG : News photographer
O over R - Owner repairman
REGISTRY - Registry of Motor Vehicles

Codes:
Regular issue passenger plates are all numeric or 3numeric - 3 alpha . Some low number plates have the month of expiration embossed. Truck and trailer plates are all numeric and captioned *commercial* or *trailer* . Some older plates which were reserved have an alpha prefix A,B,C and some have two alphas stacked as a prefix. Low numbers (under 6 characters) can be reserved for an extra fee (currently $80 for two years)

Massachusetts does not use county or weight codes on plates.
The last numeric on a regular passenger plate is an expiration code:

1- January	5. May	9. September
2. February	6. June	0. October
3. March	7. July	
4. April	8. August	

The following alpha prefixes are reserved for special use:

AMB	Ambulance
BRUINS	Member and team number
CELTICS	Member and team number
DLR	Dealer
DLR RV	Recreational vehicle dealer
EX POW	Former Prisoner of War
MD	Medical doctor
MDC	Metropolitan District Commission
NG	National Guard

Personalized plate request forms are available from Registry of Motor Vehicles,100 Nashua St., Boston, 02114. Fee is $50 per year in addition to regular registration cost. 6 alpha and/or numeric combinations allowed.

To trace the owner of a Massachusetts registered vehicle, write to the Registry at 100 Nashua St and request an abstract of the registration. The fee is $10. per record request.

MICHIGAN

STATE
ROUTE MARKER

M 43

★ WJR 760 Detroit
WCXI 1130 Detroit
WLQV 1500 Detroit
WDEY 1530 Lapeer
WCCW 1310 Traverse City

TRAVERSE CITY

LAPEER

DETROIT

AM RADIO

1 PLATE VALIDATED
BY 2 DECALS

PASSENGER REGULAR
ALSO ABC 123

PERSONALIZED 2 NEW
PLATES ISSUED EVERY YEAR

HANDICAPPED

STATE OWNED

STATE/MUNICIPAL/GOVT
& NON-PROFIT COLLEGE

COUNTY SHERIFF
VEHICLE

TRUCK-REGISTRATION BY
MAX GROSS VEHICLE
WEIGHT 24 - 61,000 LBS

TRUCK
FULL YEAR REGISTRATION

LIONS CLUB

ZONTA INTERNATIONAL
A SERVICE ORGANIZATION

FREE & ACCEPTED MASONS
A FRATERNAL ORGANIZATION

FIREMAN

PURPLE HEART
RECIPIENT

VETERAN OF
WW II

CONGRESSIONAL
MEDAL OF HONOR
RECIPIENT

54

MICHIGAN

> The "Great Lake State" issues one partially-reflectorized (glass beads on paint background) white on blue license plate. Personalized plates are re-issued annually, and in pairs.

Distinctive captions:
IN TRANSIT REPAIR: Non-dealer auto transport and service plate.
SPECIAL EQUIPMENT: Construction equipment plate.
MANUFACTURER: New untitled vehicles operated by manufacturers.
REPOSSESSION: Used by financial institutions to repossess cars
SPECIAL FARM: Farm crop transporter plate- from field to storage.
SCHOOL BUS: Non profit organization school bus, and van.
CIVIC EVENT: Parade vehicle plate.

Codes:
Michigan passenger plates are 3 alpha - 3 numeric and reverse.
The following prefixes are reserved for special use:

V	Disabled veteran	**SEN**	State senator
MSG	State owned vehicle	**25Y-29Y**	Non profit org.
REP	State Representative	**90Y**	Civil Air Patrol

The first 2 numerics on state owned plates indicate the following:

01	Highway Dept automobile
02	Highway Dept. pickup truck
03 - 05	Highway dept. heavy equipment
08, 09	Passenger vehicle state transportation pool- use by all depts.
11	Passenger vehicle assigned to individual state agency.
12, 13,16	Vehicles assigned to Dept. of Natural Resources.
71, 72	State owned vans used as small buses.

2 numerics followed by **X** - Municipal owned vehicles
All numeric characters on a plate indicates a state or government owned vehicle.

Other special prefixes:
3 numeric - **D** Auto dealer	2 numeric - **Y** Non profit org.
2 numeric - **M** Manufacturer	2 numeric - **CE** Civic event vehicle
2 numeric - **T** Transporter	2 numeric - **F** Special farm veh.
2 numeric - **R** Repossessor	2 numeric - **G** In transit repair
2 numeric - **X** Municipal	

Trucks for hire, buses and taxis have 4 numeric - 2 alpha plates.
The weight class of trucks over 24,000 lbs. GVW appears on a sticker placed at the bottom of the plate.
Trailer plates for 1 year use are: 1 alpha-5 numerics -1 alpha.
Trailers plates for 5 year use are: 1 alpha(A orB)- 5 numerics -1(A or B).

> **Personalized plates** can be ordered through any Secretary of State office located throughout the state. Any alpha/numeric combination up to a maximum of 7 characters will be considered. Fee is $25 per year plus regular registration.
>
> **To trace** the owner of a Michigan registered vehicle, write to Michigan Dept. of State, Div. of Driver & Vehicle Records, Lansing 48918. Give the plate number and request an abstract of the registration. The fee is $6.55; $7.55 for certified copies. Legislation is pending to prohibit this access.

MINNESOTA

STATE
ROUTE MARKER

MINNESOTA
95

HIBBING

MINNEAPOLIS
ST. PAUL
ROCHESTER

★ **WCCO 830** Minneapolis
WKKQ 650 Hibbing
KSTP 1500 St. Paul
KOLM 1520 Rochester

AM RADIO

EXPLORE Minnesota
123 ★ EBC
MO · 10,000 lakes · YR

2 PLATES VALIDATED
BY 2 DECALS
ON BOTH PLATES

Minnesota
LAA ★ 123
MO · 10,000 lakes · YR

PASSENGER REGULAR
EARLIER ISSUE
(STILL IN USE)

EXPLORE Minnesota
PURVIS
MO · 10,000 lakes · YR

PERSONALIZED

EXPLORE Minnesota
1234 H A
MO · 10,000 lakes · YR

HANDICAPPED PERSON
PREFIX H, HA

MINNESOTA
WX 1234
MO · YR

COURT ISSUED PLATE

MINNESOTA
T A 12 345 MO YR
10,000 lakes

FARM TRUCK PRIFIX T, OR T
PLUS ANOTHER ALPHA

MINNESOTA
Y B 12-345
MO · 10,000 lakes · YR

TRUCK NON FARM

MN **RED LAKE CHIPPEWA** 89
R L 1234
1889 · CENTENNIAL · 1989

CHIPPEWA INDIAN TRIBE
RED LAKE RESERVATION

MN FOND DU LAC BAND
12 34
LAKE SUPERIOR CHIPPEWA

CHIPPEWA INDIAN TRIBE
FOND DU LAC BAND

WHITE EARTH BAND
WE2 123
MN · CHIPPEWA INDIANS

CHIPPEWA INDIAN TRIBE
WHITE EARTH BAND

Celebrate
AH ★ 840
· MINNESOTA 1990 ·

COMMEMORATIVE PLATE

· NATIONAL GUARD ·
N G 1234
MO · MINNESOTA · YR

NATIONAL GUARD

EXPLORE Minnesota
EX POW 000
MO · 10,000 lakes · YR

FORMER PRISONER
OF WAR

BLUE ON SILVER

· WORLD WAR VET ·
W II 0123
MO · MINNESOTA · YR

WW II VETERAN

· **Minnesota** ·
PEARL HARBOR SURVIVOR **P H 007**
MO · 10,000 lakes · YR

PEARL HARBOR
SURVIVOR

COMBAT WOUNDED · VET
C W 1234
MO · MINNESOTA · YR

PURPLE HEART

The "Land of 10,000 Lakes" issues two fully-reflectorized license plates. Earlier issues do not have the state outline and the word "EXPLORE". Most non-passenger vehicle plates are non-graphic.

Distinctive captions:
CLASSIC CAR: Restored vehicles mfg.. between 1925 - 1948.
COLLECTOR: Restored vehicle mfg after 1935 at least 20 yrs old.
PIONEER: Restored vehicle mfg. prior to 1936.
TAX EXEMPT: Vehicle owned by state or political subdivision.

Codes:
Passenger plates are 3 alpha - 3 numeric and reverse. There are no county codes.
Truck and truck tractor plates are numeric and use alpha prefixes:
F over **T** - Farm trailer
Y over **A** or any combination of Y and another alpha- General purpose truck
Y over **T** - General purpose trailer
T over **L** or **M** - Farm truck with restricted highway use
T over **T**- Farm tractor
P over **R** with **L** prefix - Prorated tractor unit. The L can be other alphas.
P over **T** with **R** prefix - Prorated trailers. R can be other alphas.
C over **Z** - Trucks restricted to operation in the commercial zone of cities.
LM prefix - Commercial limousine
XW,WX,WY - Prefixes reserved for court impounded plates.

Trucks and trailer plates display weight class stickers:

Sticker code	Gross wgt in lbs.	Sticker code	Gross wgt in lbs.
E	up to 9,000	M	39,001 - 45,000
F	9,001 -12,000	N	45,001 - 51,000
G	12,001 - 15,000	O	51,001 - 57,000
H	15,001 - 18,000	P	57,001 - 63,000
I	18,001 - 21,000	Q	63,001 - 69,000
J	21,001 - 27,000	R	69,001 - 73,280
K	27,001 - 33,000	S	73,271 - 77,000
L	33,003 - 39,000	T	77,001 - 81,000
			Special permit over 81,000 lbs

Other codes
B over **Y** (prefix) - School/ charter bus
BDU - Duluth transit bus
D - Dealer
IC- Intercity bus
K- Citizen's band radio call sign
R - Recreational vehicle
S over **B** - Contract school bus

2 C - Transit bus
WX,WY,XW- Special plate issued by a court when owner has been convicted and the original plates impounded. These plates permit law enforcement to stop and inspect the vehicle and driver at any time.(Often used in cases of DUI).

Personalized plate request forms are available from any deputy registrar, or by mail from Div. of Motor Vehicles Dept of Transportation Bldg.. St.Paul 55155. 1 - 7 character may be requested. The fee is $100 plus registration.

To trace the owner write of Driver and Vehicle Services Div. Transportation Bldg. St. Paul 55155. Give the plate number and the fee is $4.00 per record. Add $1.00 for a previous owner information and/or certified copy.

MISSISSIPPI

STATE ROUTE MARKER
50

WSLI 930 Jackson
WMER 1390 Meridian
WQBC 1420 Vicksburg
WROA 1390 Gulfport

JACKSON
VICKSBURG
MERIDIAN
GULFPORT

AM RADIO

MISSISSIPPI
1ABC123
HINDS
1 PLATE VALIDATED
BY 2 DECALS

MISSISSIPPI
RIVER
HINDS
PERSONALIZED

MISSISSIPPI
123
100% DAV
DISABLED VETERAN

MISSISSIPPI
UNITED STATES
ARMED FORCES
RETIRED 9AC
NAVY
RETIRED NAVY VETERAN

MISSISSIPPI
S - 2345
STATE PROPERTY
STATE OWNED

MISSISSIPPI
TAX EXMPT M 1234
CITY
MUNICIPAL OWNED

OCT MISSISSIPPI 92
P 26 601
PRIVATE COMMERCIAL
TRUCK 26,000 LBS

OCT MISSISSIPPI 92
H 72 1234
FOR HIRE TRUCK
72,000

OCT MISSISSIPPI 92
F 16 1234
FARM TRUCK
16,000

DEC MISSISSIPPI 92
810001P
APPORTIONED
INTERSTATE TRUCK
80,000LBS

MISSISSIPPI
NC BUS 55
NON COMMERCIAL BUS
5 YR. TAG

OCT MISSISSIPPI 92
C C BUS 123
COMMON CARRIER BUS

OCT MISSISSIPPI 92
TLR 1234
TRUCK TRAILER

MISSISSIPPI
P 50 1234 6 92
TEMPORARY
FARM VEHICLE
3-6 MONTH USE

MISSISSIPPI
2345
NATIONAL GUARD
NATIONAL GUARD
5 YR PLATE

MISSISSIPPI
Antique Car 1210
VEHICLE
25 YEARS OLD

MISSISSIPPI

"The Magnolia State issues one fully-reflectorized license plate. The county name is embossed on all passenger and light truck plates.

Distinctive captions:
ANTIQUE CAR- A vehicle 25 years or older.
100% DAV - Veteran totally disabled - service connected.
NC BUS - Non-commercial bus.
TAX FREE- Municipal government vehicle
TEMPORARY FARM - 3 - 6 month vehicle registration.

Codes:
Private passenger car plates have 3 alpha - 3 numeric characters and the county of origin appears on the bottom of the plate. The alpha numeric combinations are for individual vehicle identification only and have no hidden codes.

State officials and state owned vehicles have the following codes:

1 - Governor
2 - Lt. Governor
X1, X2 - Former Gov, & Lt, Gov.
(Prefix) **SO** - Sheriff's office.
(**1** is Sheriff, **2** and up deputies)

X US CONGRESS - Former rep.
X US SENATE - Former senator

State owned vehicles have permanent plates. All vehicles are issued the same type tag in numerical sequence. There are no hidden codes.

Trucks, truck tractors, trailers and other commercial vehicles have an alpha numeric prefix on the left side of the plate. the alpha indicates the use and the numeric the weight class in thousands of pounds.

CC - Common carrier bus
F - Farm vehicle(hauling own property)
H - Truck for hire.
H - BUS - Vehicle for hire (max 7 pass.)
H - DRAY - Truck for hire (5 mile area).

HH - Moving van for hire.
NC - BUS - Non commercial bus
P - Private commercial vehicle (haul own)
TLR - Trailer

The following numerics appear immediately following the alpha prefix and indicate the gross vehicle weight in thousands of pounds:

10	26	40	46	52	58	64	72	78
16	30	42	48	54	60	66	74	80-
20	36	44	50	56	62	68	76	max

Pickup truck up to 6000 lbs plates begin with the numeric 8 - alpha - numerics, up to 10,000 lbs are Numeric 9 - alpha - 4 numerics. The county name appears.

Personalized plate applications available at county tax offices. 1 - 6 characters permitted. Fee $15 per yr. plus other taxes for a five year plate.

To trace a plate write Miss. State Tax Commission, attn Motor Vehicle Licensing Div .PO. Box 1140 Jackson MS 39215. Fee is $1.00 per request.

MISSOURI

WHITE ON MAROON

JAN MISSOURI
AAB · 123
YR
SHOW-ME STATE

2 PLATES VALIDATED BY
1 DECAL IN
CENTER OF BOTH PLATES

STATE ROUTE MARKER

17

KANSAS CITY
ST. LOUIS

★ **KMOX 1120** St. Louis
KXEN 1010 St. Louis
KCMO 810 Kansas City
WHB 710 Kansas City

AM RADIO

JUL MISSOURI YR
TWAIN
SHOW-ME STATE

PERSONALIZED
(2 PLATES)

SEP MISSOURI
2 · AAA
YR
SHOW-ME STATE

HANDICAPPED

MISSOURI
123
OFFICIAL CAR

STATE OWNED VEHICLE

JAN L 6 MO
AAO · 123
YR
SHOW-ME STATE

LOCAL TRUCK
6-12,000 LBS

JAN BL9 MO
JZ9 · 123
YR
6 APPORTIONED

BEYOND LOCAL TRUCK
9,000 LBS

MISSOURI
ZT9 · 123
YR
6 APPORTIONED

APPORTIONED TRUCK
6-12,000 LBS

JAN MO
12345
CENTRAL MISSOURI STATE UNIVERSITY

COLLEGIATE PLATE
CENTRAL MISSOURI
STATE UNIVERSITY

OCT MO
12345
SAINT LOUIS UNIVERSITY

COLLEGIATE PLATE
SAINT LOUIS UNIVERSITY

OCT MO
OZARK
COLLEGE OF THE OZARKS

COLLEGIATE PLATE
COLLEGE OF THE OZARKS

SEP BL 12 MO
100 · OAR
YR
ARMY RESERVE

ARMY RESERVE

JUL MO
FLORA
HISTORIC VEHICLE

HISTORIC VEHICLE

OCT MISSOURI
100 · 1PW
YR
FORMER P O W

FORMER
PRISONER OF WAR

JAN MISSOURI YR
C - O
HONORARY CONSUL

HONORARY
CONSUL

SEP YR MO
PEARL
HARBOR
SURVIVOR
123
SHOW-ME STATE

PEARL HARBOR SURVIVOR

MISSOURI JUL
**CONGRESSIONAL
MEDAL of HONOR**
1

MEDAL OF HONOR
RECIPIENT

MISSOURI

The "Show Me State" issues two partially-reflectorized license plates (glass beads on paint background).The expiration decal on passenger plates appears in the middle of the each plate.

Distinctive captions:
SHOW-ME-STATE- State nickname
DRIVE AWAY - Transporter plate (other than dealer).
HISTORIC VEHICLE - Restored vehicle over 25 yrs old.
OFFICIAL CAR - State owned vehicle

Codes:
Passenger license plates have 3 alpha - 3 numeric characters.
The first alpha indicates the month of expiration:

A, V - Jan.	**G, H** - MAY	**Q, Z** - Dec
B, D - Feb.	**J, K** - JUN.	**S, W** - SEP.
C, L - Mar.	**M, N** - JUL.	**X, T** - OCT
E, F - APR.	**P, R** - AUG.	PERSONALIZED - JUL.

Other codes-
D - Dealer
DV - Disabled Veteran
HP - State Highway Patrol
R - State Representative
S - State Senator
USS, USC - US Senate, Congress

Missouri does not indicate county or origin on license plates.

Truck plates are issued to all motor vehicles used for transportation of property. Fees are based on gross weight (combined weight of the vehicle and the load) and zone of operation either local or beyond.
Truck, trailer and bus codes that appear on the top or bottom of the plate:

L - (Local)Limited to a municipality
and 25 miles beyond
BL - Can operate beyond local area
Apportioned - Interstate operator
L BUS - Local bus, 25 mile area
T BUS - Transit bus
C BUS - Commercial bus

The small numeric that appears in conjunction with the above codes indicates the weight class for trucks, and number of passengers for transit and commercial buses.
Trucks in the 12,000 lb. and under class are issued plates with and alpha expiration code the same as passenger plates. Heavier truck and bus plates are all numeric:
100,001 - 400,000 local, 500,001 - 800,000 beyond local

Personalized plates are available from any Motor Vehicle and Drivers Licensing Bureau. Up to 6 characters will be considered. Fee is $15 per yr.plus registration .

To trace the owner write to Missouri Dept. of Revenue, Motor Vehicle and Drivers Licensing Bureau, Jefferson City 65105. Request an abstract of the registration.Enclose a $4.00 fee for this service.

MONTANA

5·1234A

2 PLATES VALIDATED
BY 1 DECAL
ON BOTH PLATES

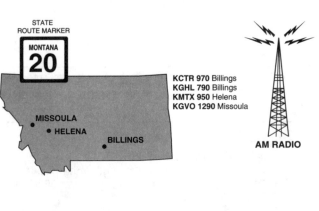

STATE
ROUTE MARKER

MONTANA
20

MISSOULA
HELENA
BILLINGS

KCTR 970 Billings
KGHL 790 Billings
KMTX 950 Helena
KGVO 1290 Missoula

AM RADIO

1AAA12
100 YEARS MONTANA

PASSENGER - MONTANA
CENTENNIAL PLATE
VALID UNTIL 12/31/96

LAZY K

PERSONALIZED

12345

DISABLED

MPH·123

HIGHWAY PATROL

EXEMPT
12·1234
MONTANA

COUNTY OWNED VEHICLE

12T·1234

TRUCK LAST 4 CHARACTERS
CAN BE 1 ALPHA-3 NUMERIC

12 TR 1234

TRAILER

APPORTIONED
P·1207
MONTANA

APPORTIONED VEHICLE

123
PIONEER MONTANA

COLLECTOR'S VEHICLE

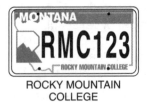

NMC123
NORTHERN MONTANA COLLEGE

NORTHERN MONTANA
COLLEGE

RMC123
ROCKY MOUNTAIN COLLEGE

ROCKY MOUNTAIN
COLLEGE

UMC123
University of Montana

UNIVERSITY OF MONTANA

12345

VETERAN (COAST GUARD)

12345

VETERAN (MARINE)

NG 1234

NATIONAL GUARD

"Big Sky Country" issues two fully-reflectorized license plates. The numeric prefix indicates the county or origin. Centennial plates are available trough 1996.

Distinctive captions:
EXEMPT - County owned vehicle
PIONEER - Vehicle manufactured in 1933 or earlier.
VINTAGE - Vehicle more than 30 yrs. old, mfg.1934 or later.

Codes:
The first 2 numeric characters on passenger ,truck and large trailer plates is a county code.Passenger plates under 10 have an alpha P. The county code and (county seats) are:

1P - Silver Bow (Butte)	20 - Valley (Glasgow)	39 - Fallon -(Baker)
2P - Cascade (Great Falls)	21 - Toole (Shelby)	40 - Sweet Grass (Big Timber)
3P - Yellowstone (Billings)	22 - Big Horn (Hardin)	41 - McCone (Circle)
4P - Missoula (Missoula)	23 - Musselshell (Roundup)	42 - Carter (Ekalaka)
5P - Lewis & Clark(Helena)	24 - Blaine (Chinook)	43 - Broadwater (Townsend)
6P - Gallatin (Bozeman)	25 - Madison (Virginia City)	44 - Wheatland (Harlowton)
7P - Flathead (Kalispell)	26 - Pondera (Conrad)	45 - Prairie (Terry)
8P - Fergus (Lewistown)	27 - Richland (Sidney)	46 - Granite (Philipsburg)
9P - Powder River (Broadus)	28 - Powell (Deer Lodge)	47 - Meagher (Whte Sul Spgs)
10 - Carbon (Red Lodge)	29 - Rosebud (Forsyth)	48 - Liberty (Chester)
11 - Phillips - (Malta)	30 - Deer Lodge (Anaconda)	49 - Park (Livingston)
12 - Hill (Havre)	31 - Teton (Chouteau)	50 - Garfield (Jordan)
13 - Ravalli (Hamilton)	32 - Stillwater (Columbus)	51 - Jefferson (Boulder)
14 - Custer (Miles City)	33 - Treasure (Hysham)	52 - Wibaux (Wibaux)
15 - Lake (Polson)	34 - Sheridan (Plentywood)	53 - Golden Valley (Ryegate)
16 - Dawson (Glendive)	35 - Sanders (ThompsonFalls)	54 - Mineral (Superior)
17 - Roosevelt (Wolf Pt.)	36 - Judith Basin (Stanford)	55 - Petroleum (Winnett)
18 - Beaverhead (Dillon)	37 - Daniels (Scobey)	56 - Lincoln (Libby)
19 - Chouteau (Ft. Benton)	38 - Glacier (Cut Bank)	

Alpha characters indicate the following:

DS	Driver service	**D**	Dealer
FG	Fish & Game Comm.	**UD**	Used car dealer
H	State Highway Dept.	**P** (prefix)	Truck tractor (Power)
M	State owned vehicle	**T**	Truck
MHP	MT. Highway Patrol	**T** over **R**	Trailer
MSP	MT. State Prison		

Montana does not designate the weight of a vehicle on the license plate.

Personalized plates are available through County Treasurers offices. The fee is initially $25 in addition to the regular registration fee.Renewal is $10. 2 - 7 alpha and/or numerics will be considered.

To trace the owner of a vehicle write to Montana Dept. of Justice, Registrar's Office, Motor Vehicle Div., Deer Lodge 59722. The fee for owner information is $3.00 per inquiry, and owner and lien information $6. Use this address requesting samples.

NEBRASKA

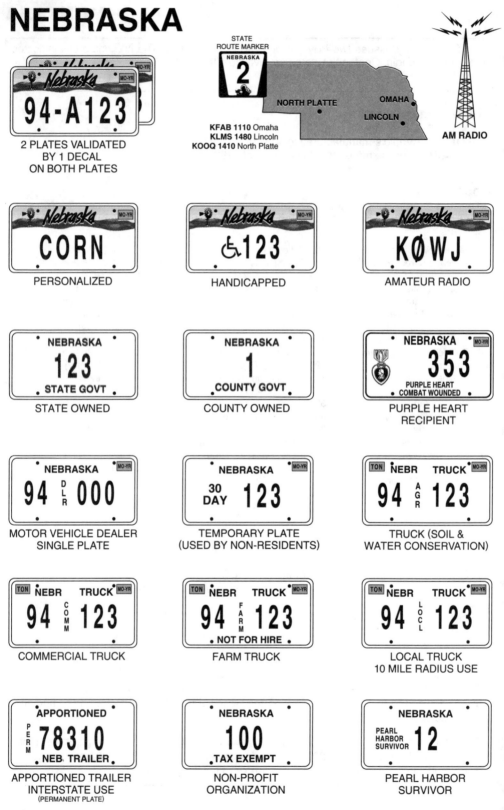

STATE ROUTE MARKER

NEBRASKA 2

NORTH PLATTE • OMAHA
LINCOLN •

KFAB 1110 Omaha
KLMS 1480 Lincoln
KOOQ 1410 North Platte

AM RADIO

94-A123

2 PLATES VALIDATED
BY 1 DECAL
ON BOTH PLATES

CORN

PERSONALIZED

♿123

HANDICAPPED

KØWJ

AMATEUR RADIO

NEBRASKA
123
STATE GOVT

STATE OWNED

NEBRASKA
1
COUNTY GOVT

COUNTY OWNED

NEBRASKA
353
PURPLE HEART
COMBAT WOUNDED

PURPLE HEART
RECIPIENT

NEBRASKA
94 DLR 000

MOTOR VEHICLE DEALER
SINGLE PLATE

NEBRASKA
30 DAY 123

TEMPORARY PLATE
(USED BY NON-RESIDENTS)

TON NEBR TRUCK
94 AGR 123

TRUCK (SOIL &
WATER CONSERVATION)

TON NEBR TRUCK
94 COMM 123

COMMERCIAL TRUCK

TON NEBR TRUCK
94 FARM 123
NOT FOR HIRE

FARM TRUCK

TON NEBR TRUCK
94 LOCL 123

LOCAL TRUCK
10 MILE RADIUS USE

APPORTIONED
PERM 78310
NEB. TRAILER

APPORTIONED TRAILER
INTERSTATE USE
(PERMANENT PLATE)

NEBRASKA
100
TAX EXEMPT

NON-PROFIT
ORGANIZATION

NEBRASKA
PEARL HARBOR SURVIVOR **12**

PEARL HARBOR
SURVIVOR

64

NEBRASKA

The "Cornhusker State" issues two fully-reflectorized license plates. The numeric prefix indicates the county of origin. Nebraska generally replaces all plates every 3 years with the exception of: Government, Tax Exempt and Historical plates which are considered permanent. A complete new issue of plates will begin Jan. 1993.

Distinctive captions:
APP - Apportioned
COMM - Commercial vehicles for hire and equipped to carry cargo.
LOCL - Commercial vehicle , 10 mile area of operations.
HISTORICAL - A restored vehicle 30 years or older.
R - Repossession plate used by finance companies.
T - Transporter of vehicles not their own, for delivery.

BX -Boat dealer
FV - Movie or tv production vehicle

Codes:
Nebraska passenger vehicle license plates have a numeric county prefix followed by an alpha and numerics. Truck plates have the same county prefix followed by captions **COMM**, **LOCAL**, **FARM** and **AGR**.

The county prefixes and (County seats) are as follows:

Codes County (Seat)

1 - Douglas (Omaha)	32 - Thayer (Hebron)	63 - Boyd (Butte)
2 - Lancaster (Lincoln)	33 - Jefferson (Fairbury)	64 - Morrill (Bridgeport)
3 - Gage (Beatrice)	34 - Fillmore (Geneva)	65 - Box Butte (Alliance)
4 - Custer (Broken Bow)	35 - Dixon (Ponca)	66 - Cherry (Valentine)
5 - Dodge (Fremont)	36 - Holt (O'Neill)	67 - Hitchcock (Trenton)
6 - Saunders (Wahoo)	37 - Phelps (Holdrege)	68 - Keith (Ogallala)
7 - Madison (Madison)	38 - Furnas (Beaver City)	69 - Dawes ((Chadron)
8 - Hall (Grand Island)	39 - Cheyenne (Sidney)	70 - Dakota (Dakota City)
9 - Buffalo (Kearney)	40 - Pierce (Pierce)	71 - Kimball (Kimball)
10 - Platte (Columbus)	41 - Polk (Osceola)	72 - Chase (Imperial)
11 - Otoe (Nebraska City)	42 - Nuckolls (Nelson)	73 - Gosper (Elwood)
12 - Knox (Center)	43 - Colfax (Schuyler)	74 - Perkins (Grant)
13 - Cedar (Hartington)	44 - Nemaha (Auburn)	75 - Brown (Ainsworth)
14 - Adams (Hastings)	45 - Webster (Red Cloud)	76 - Dundy (Benkelman)
15 - Lincoln (North Platte)	46 - Merrick (CentralCity)	77 - Garden (Oshkosh)
16 - Seward (Seward)	47 - Valley (Ord)	78- Deuel (Chappell)
17 - York (York)	48 - Red Willow (McCook)	79 -Hayes (Hayes Center)
18 - Dawson (Dawson)	49 - Howard (St. Paul)	80 - Sioux (Harrison)
19 - Richardson (Falls Cty)	50 - Franklin (Franklin)	81 - Rock - (Bassett)
20 - Cass (Plattsmouth)	51 - Harlan (Alma)	82 - Keya Paha (Springview.)
21 - Scotts Bluff (Gering)	52 - Kearney (Minden)	83 - Garfield (Burwell)
22 - Saline (Wilber)	53 - Stanton (Stanton)	84 - Wheeler (Bartlett)
23 - Boone (Albion)	54 - Pawnee (Pawnee City)	85 - Banner (Harrisburg)
24 - Cuming (West Point)	55 - Thurston (Pender)	86 - Blaine (Brewster)
25 - Butler (David City)	56 - Sherman (Loup City)	87 - Logan (Stapleton)
26 - Antelope (Neligh)	57 - Johnson (Tecumseh)	88 - Loup (Taylor)
27 - Wayne (Wayne)	58 - Nance (Fullerton)	89 - Thomas (Thedford)
28 - Hamilton (Aurora)	59 - Sarpy (Papillion)	90 - McPherson (Tryon)
29 - Washington (Blair)	60 - Frontier (Stockville)	91 - Arthur (Arthur)
30 - Clay (Clay Center)	61 - Sheridan (Rushville)	92 - Grant (Hyannis)
31 - Burt (Tekamah)	62 - Greeley (Greeley)	93 - Hooker (Mullen)

All Nebraska registered trucks carry a tonnage sticker on their license plate.

Personalized plate request forms are available from Registration Division, Dept of Motor Vehicles, State Capital, Lincoln 68509. Fee is $75 and renewal is $35 in addition to regular county fee. Up to 7 alpha numerics can be used.

To trace the owner of a Nebraska vehicle, write to Titles and Registration, Motor Vehicles Division, Lincoln 68509.

NEVADA

2 PLATES VALIDATED BY
1 DECAL ON
THE REAR PLATE

STATE
ROUTE MARKER

KROW 780 Reno
KDWN 720 Las Vegas
KROL 870 Laughlin
KVLV 980 Fallon

AM RADIO

COMMEMORATIVE PLATE
ISSUED 10-1-89
STILL IN USE

PASSENGER OLDER ISSUE
COUNTY STICKER OPTIONAL

PASSENGER
FIRST ISSUED 1970
OLDER ISSUE STILL IN USE

PASSENGER
FIRST ISSUED 1974
OLDER ISSUE STILL IN USE

PERSONALIZED

HANDICAPPED

TAX EXEMPT
STATE/CITY/COUNTY
OWNED

TRUCK

TRAILER

INTERSTATE TRUCK
PRORATED

DEALER

MEMBER OF PRESS

PEARL HARBOR
SURVIVOR

NATIONAL GUARD
MEMBER

FORMER PRISONER
OF WAR

66

NEVADA

The "Silver State" issues two fully-reflective license plates. The last general re-issue of plates was in 1969. Since then 7 styles of plates have been issued and are still used.

Distinctive captions:

E X - Tax exempt (State / city / county) vehicle
DOT- Nevada Dept. of Transportation
OLD TIMER - Collector's veh. 40 yrs. or older.
HORSELESS CARRIAGE - Collector's veh. 1915 or older.

BODY SHOP
Loaner plate used by shop.

Codes:

Starting in 1982, new Nevada plates have 3 alpha- 3 numeric characters. The older series of passenger plates with an alpha county code prefix are still in use. These codes are:

C, CA - CZ, (no CH) CAA - CZZ: Clark(Las Vegas)
CH, CHA - CHZ: Churchill (Fallon)
DAA - DZZ, DS, Douglas(Minden)
EAA - EZZ, EL, ELA - ELZ: Elko (Elko)
ES, ESA - ESZ: Esmeralda (Goldfield)
EU, EUA - EUZ: Eureka (Eureka)
FAA, FZZ: Churchill (Fallon)
HU, HUA - HUZ: Humboldt (Winnemucca)
KAA - KZZ: Washoe (Reno)
LA, LAA - LAZ: Lander (Austin)
LN, LNA - LNZ: Lincoln (Pioche)

LY, LYA - LYZ, LBB - LZZ: Lyon (Yearington)
MAA - MZZ, MN, MNA - MNZ: Mineral(Hawthorne)
NAA - NZZ, NY, NYA - NYZ: Nye(Tonopah)
OAA - OZZ, OR, ORA - ORZ: Ormsby (Carson City)
PAA - PZZ, PE, PEAPPEZ: Pershing (Lovelock)
ST, STA - STZ: Storey (Virginia City)
TAA -TZZ: Clark (Las Vegas)
W, WAA - WZZ: Washoe (Reno)
WP, WPA - WPZ: White Pine (Ely)
ZAA - ZZZ: White Pine (Ely)

Truck and truck tractor plates issued before 1982 have a county prefix code:

AA - AZ Churchill	**GA - GZ** Eureka	**MA - MZ** Mineral	**WA - WZ** Washoe
BA - BZ Clark	**HA - HZ** Humboldt	**OA - OZ** Carson City	**YA - YZ** Clark
DA - DZ Douglas	**JAPJZ** Lander	**NA - NZ** Nye	**ZA - ZZ** White Pine
EA - EZ Elko	**KA - KZ** Lincoln	**PA - PZ** Pershing	
FA - FZ Esmeralda	**LB - LZ** Lyon	**SA - SZ** Storey	

Trailer plates issued before 1982 have 1 alpha- 5 numeric characters. The current issue plate format is reversed. There are no county or weight codes.
The following suffix and prefixes have special significance:

P - Prorated truck registration fee (Interstate operation)
T - Prorated trailer registration fee (Interstate operation)

Nevada requires all trucks over 5,000 lbs to display Motor Carrier Tax plate in addition to vehicle registration plates. The tax codes are:

Suffix **B** - 2 axle trucks under 10,000 lbs operating 50 mi. either side CA NV border.
C - Truck permitted to operate only within city limit and 5 miles beyond
M - Indicates Weight Fee or Mileage tax method of payment.
V - A convoy plate issued to transport vehicles.
X - Indicates mileage tax method of payment

Nevada does not indicate the weight class of a truck, tractor or trailer by any code on the registration plate.

Personalized plate forms are available form Div. of Motor Vehicles, 555 Wright Way, Carson City 89711. A maximum of 7 alpha numeric characters permitted. Initial fee is $25, $15 annual renewal in addition to regular registration cost.

To trace the owner of a vehicle write to: DMV Record Section, 555 Wright Way, Carson City, 89711. Give the legal reason for the request. The fee is $3.00.

NEW HAMPSHIRE

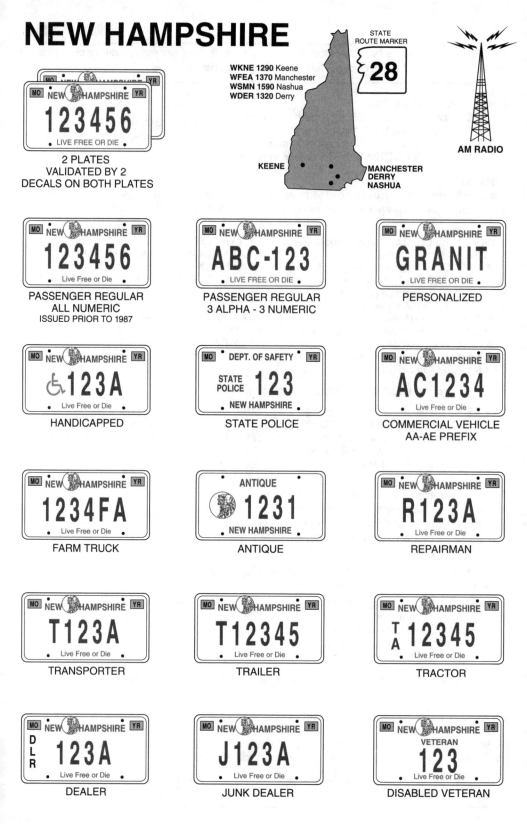

STATE ROUTE MARKER

28

WKNE 1290 Keene
WFEA 1370 Manchester
WSMN 1590 Nashua
WDER 1320 Derry

KEENE

MANCHESTER
DERRY
NASHUA

AM RADIO

123456
LIVE FREE OR DIE

2 PLATES
VALIDATED BY 2
DECALS ON BOTH PLATES

123456
Live Free or Die

PASSENGER REGULAR
ALL NUMERIC
ISSUED PRIOR TO 1987

ABC-123
LIVE FREE OR DIE

PASSENGER REGULAR
3 ALPHA - 3 NUMERIC

GRANIT
LIVE FREE OR DIE

PERSONALIZED

123A
Live Free or Die

HANDICAPPED

DEPT. OF SAFETY
STATE POLICE **123**
NEW HAMPSHIRE

STATE POLICE

AC1234
Live Free or Die

COMMERCIAL VEHICLE
AA-AE PREFIX

1234FA
Live Free or Die

FARM TRUCK

ANTIQUE
1231
NEW HAMPSHIRE

ANTIQUE

R123A
Live Free or Die

REPAIRMAN

T123A
Live Free or Die

TRANSPORTER

T12345
Live Free or Die

TRAILER

T A 12345
Live Free or Die

TRACTOR

D L R 123A
Live Free or Die

DEALER

J123A
Live Free or Die

JUNK DEALER

VETERAN
123
Live Free or Die

DISABLED VETERAN

68

The "Granite State" issues two fully-reflectorized license plates with the unique slogan "Live Free or Die". Two different numbering systems are in use for passenger plates. Earlier issue plates are all numeric, while the current issue is three alpha - three numeric.

Distinctive captions:

JUDICIAL - Judge, Supreme Court, Superior Court.
PERMANENT- County, city or town owned vehicle.
SHERIFF (1-10) - Sheriff of one of New Hampshire's 10 counties.
SHERIFF DEPT - Deputies and staff
VETERAN - Disabled veteran

Codes:

Private passenger cars are issued green on white plates with all numeric characters and there are no county codes.

Commercial and special class vehicle plates or alpha and numeric. They contain no county or weight codes, but the alpha character indicates as follows:

Prefix

A - All commercial plates begin with A
AMB - Ambulance
J - Junk dealer
R - Licensed repairman
SB - School bus
T - Transporter or trailer
T over A - Tractor
U - Utility dealer plate

Suffix

AG - Agricultural vehicle highway use limited to within 20 miles of farm.
AN - Collector's veh.at least 25 yrs old.
FA - Farm vehicle- unlimited highway use.
T - Trailer

State government vehicle plates have an alpha prefix that is a department code:

A - Administration	**ES** - Water Supply Control	**P** - Public health
AE - Aeronautics	**F** - Fish & game	**S** - Safety
AGR - Agriculture	**M** - General code for	**SW** - Sweepstakes
B - Banking	Depts with few veh.	**T** - Tax
C - Civil Defense	**H** - Highway	**TR** - Trailers
COR - Prison Industries	**L** - Liquor	**U** - University system
D - Recreation & Economics	**LA** - Labor	**Y** - Industrial
E - Education	**NG** - National Guard	

Personalized plate request forms are available at any Motor Vehicle Div. office. Any combination of a maximum of 6 alpha or numeric characters will be considered. Fee $25 per year in addition to regular registration cost.

To trace the owner of a plate write to NH Motor Vehicle Div., Concord 03305 and request an abstract of the registration . Fee is $2 per request.

NEW JERSEY

STATE ROUTE MARKER

3

MORRISTOWN

PRINCETON

TRENTON

WMID 1340 Atlantic City
WBUD 1260 Trenton
WHWH 1350 Princeton
WMTR 1250 Morristown

ATLANTIC CITY

AM RADIO

NEW JERSEY
123 ABC
GARDEN STATE

2 PLATES PASSENGER
VALIDATED BY
STICKER ON WINDOW

New Jersey
AAA 1234
Garden State

NEW ISSUE 1992

N.J.
ABC-123
GARDEN STATE

PASSENGER OLDER ISSUE
NJ CAN ALSO APPEAR
AS NEW JERSEY

NEW JERSEY
GDM 1
GARDEN STATE

COURTESY PLATE
INITIALS & LOW NUMBERS 1-20

NEW JERSEY
HA 1234
GARDEN STATE

HANDICAPPED

GARDEN STATE
A 1 NJ
SENATE

STATE SENATOR

NEW JERSEY
A 4 TM
COUNTY OFFICER

COUNTY OFFICER
PREFIX: COUNTY CODE
SUFFIX: OWNERS INITIALS

STATE GOVT
SG A123
N.J.

STATE OWNED

NEW JERSEY
TP A123
GARDEN STATE

N.J. TURNPIKE AUTHORITY

MUNICIPAL
MG A123
N.J.

CITY OWNED

COMMERCIAL
XA 12BC
N.J. MO-YR

COMMERCIAL VEHICLES
VALIDATED BY
PLATE DECALS

TRAILER
TWR 123
N.J. MO-YR

TRAILERS

FARMER
XYZ 123
N.J. MO-YR

FARMER OWNED VEHICLE

NEW JERSEY
JWM CMH

CONGRESSIONAL
MEDAL OF HONOR
RECIPIENT'S INITIALS

NEW JERSEY
1000 PH
PEARL HARBOR 41

PEARL HARBOR
SURVIVOR

NEW JERSEY
MC 1000
LEATHERNECK

MARINE CORPS
LEAGUE

70

The "Garden State" will phase in a new reflectorized base plate starting in mid 1992. all non-reflectorized plates currently in use will be replaced by 1997. Passenger cars will continue to be issued 2 plates validated by windshield decal, however spaces are included in the new design for plate decals.

Distinctive captions:

CONSTRUCTOR - Construction veh. under 70,000 lbs.
COMMERCIAL - Non-passenger veh. used for business.
FARMER - Used to carry produce, not for hire.
FARM USE - Farm machinery, limited highway use
FIREFIGHTER - Fireman
FIRST AIDER - Medic
HISTORIC - Exhibition vehicle 25 yrs old.
IN TRANSIT - Road building equipment in transit.
LIVERY - licensed limousine.
MV INSPECTOR - Motor Vehicle Dept. law enforcement.
NON CONV DLR - Non conventional vehicle dealer.
OMNIBUS - Vehicle for hire (bus, taxi)
PUC-LIM - Limousine authorized by Public Utility Comm.
SCHOOL VEH I - School veh 16 or more passengers.
SCHOOL VEH II - School veh. less than 16 pass.
SOLID WASTE-Vehicles used to transport solid waste.
TEMP R - L - Rental company transporter plate.
TRACTOR - Traction or tractor, well drilling machine plates
VEH. CONV. - Converters of commercial vehicles

Other captions:

AIR GUARD
ASSEMBLY
ARMY GUARD
ARMY RESERVE
CABINET
CHIROPRACTOR
COMMUTER VAN
COUNTY OFFICER
DENTIST
DISABLED VET
FREEHOLDER
NEW CAR DLR
PHYSICIAN
PODIATRIST
POW
STREET ROD
TEMPORARY
USAF RESERVE
USCG RESERVE
USMC RESERVE
USN RESERVE
USED CAR DLR
VEHICLE MFR

Codes:

New Jersey issues 3 alpha - 3 numeric, 3 numeric -3 alpha, 3 alpha - 2 numeric-1 alpha plates (3-2-1 system) to passenger vehicles. Courtesy plates (reserved number series) have a maximum of 5 characters, usually 3 alpha either preceded or followed by 1 or 2 numerics below the number 20.There is a $15 courtesy plate fee.
New Jersey issues collegiate plates to alumni groups too numerous to list here, but include such institutions as Rutgers and Penn State.

Reserved prefixes

DAV	Disabled veteran	**NJP**	New Jersey Press
DTF	Repossessor plate	**NYP**	New York Press
DTT	Manufacturer transporter	**TD**	NJ Dept. of Transportation
HA	Gdn. St. Parkway Auth.	**TP**	NJ Turnpike Authority
NF	No fee (non profit org.)		

Small numeric characters embossed on the right side of a plate indicates the number of plates issued to an individual or company on the same registration.

New Jersey does not designate county of origin or weight on license plates.

Personalized plates applications are available for Motor Vehicle Div., Special Plate Unit CN015, Trenton 08666. The extra fee is $50 and 3 - 7 characters are allowed. (Use this address for samples).

To trace the owner of a New Jersey vehicle, write to NJ Div. of Motor Vehicles, Certified Information Unit, 120 Stockton St., Trenton. Give the plate number and request an abstract of the registration. The fee is $5.00 payable by certified check.

NEW MEXICO

STATE ROUTE MARKER

6

FARMINGTON

ALBUQUERQUE

KDEF 1150 Albuquerque
KKIM 1000 Albuquerque
KKOB 770 Albuquerque
KENN 1390 Farmington

AM RADIO

SANTA FE
001 AAB
New Mexico USA
Land of Enchantment · MO/YR

PASSENGER
(NEW ISSUE JAN 91)
PLATE IS VALIDATED
BY 1 DECAL

SANTA FE
KAK 001
New Mexico USA
Land of Enchantment · MO/YR

PASSENGER
THIS & ALL PREVIOUS
BASES TO BE
REPLACED BY JULY 1,1993

SANTA FE
PIÑON
New Mexico USA
Land of Enchantment · MO/YR

PRESTIGE PLATE

BERNALILLO
V T 0469
ARMED FORCES VETERAN
NEW MEXICO · MO/YR

ARMED FORCES VETERAN

BERNALILLO
T R A 3143
New Mexico USA
Land of Enchantment · MO/YR

TRAILER

DONA ANA
347 ANG
NATIONAL GUARD
NEW MEXICO · MO/YR

NATIONAL GUARD

TAOS
MOUNTED PATROL 4 11
LAND OF ENCHANTMENT
NEW MEXICO · MO/YR

MOUNTED PATROL AUXILIARY
POLICE ORGANIZATION

W D 23134
LAND OF ENCHANTMENT
NEW MEXICO · MO/YR

WEIGHT DISTANCE
TRUCK PLATE

P R 14299
LAND OF ENCHANTMENT
NEW MEXICO · MO/YR

PRORATE TRUCK PLATE

BERNALILLO
0088 H P
HANDICAPPED
· New Mexico USA · MO/YR

HANDICAPPED

XM17836
LAND OF ENCHANTMENT
NEW MEXICO · MO/YR

EXEMPT MUNICIPAL
(CITY OWNED)

U S REP1 3
U.S. REPRESENTATIVE
NEW MEXICO · MO/YR

U.S. REPRESENTATIVE
(S.S. STATE SENATE)

VALENCIA
EX-PRISONER
OF WAR 247
LAND OF ENCHANTMENT
NEW MEXICO · MO/YR

FORMER PRISONER OF WAR

0039
PURPLE HEART
NEW MEXICO · MO/YR

PURPLE HEART
RECIPIENT

VALENCIA
041
PEARL HARBOR SURVIVOR
NEW MEXICO · MO/YR

PEARL HARBOR SURVIVOR

BERNALILO
LRR 1
MEDAL OF HONOR
NEW MEXICO · MO/YR

MEDAL OF HONOR
(INITIALS OF RECIPIENT)

The "Land of Enchantment" issues one fully-reflectorized license plate. New Mexico is in the midst of its first general plate re-issue since 1972, with the new graphic format plate scheduled to replace the previous bases by 1993.

Distinctive captions:

MOUNTED PATROL -Statewide auxiliary police organization
NM RANGER-Auxiliary police organization
HORSELESS CARRIAGE - Vehicle at least 35 years old.
DISABLED VETERAN - 100% disabled combat veteran.

Codes:

Most recent issue New Mexico passenger and light truck plates are 3 numeric - 3 alpha. Previous issues were 3 alpha- 3 numeric plates to passenger cars. Trucks and most other commercial vehicles have a 2 alpha prefix followed by 4 numerics. The county of origin name appears at the top of all (except official) new format plates, however this is not enforced.

Prefixes indicate as follows:

A - New cycle plate prefix	**PR** - Prorated vehicle
DE - Driver education	**R** - State representative
D over L - Dealer	**R over V** - Recreational vehicle
F over L - Fleet registration	**SB, SBA** - School bus
F over R - Freight trailer	**S**- State senator
FT- Farm truck	**T- HD** - Highway Dept. trailer
HD - Highway Dept	**T over R** - Trailer
H over P - Handicapped	**TX** - Taxi
HT -Highway & Transportation	**US** - U.S. Govt.; Indian Agency vehicles
I over R - Apportioned	**WD** - Weight distance (Interstate vehicles)
M over H - Mobile home	**WR** - Wrecker
N over G - National Guard	**WS** - Wholesaler
OF - State owned vehicle	**XC** - County government
PB - Private bus	**XM** - City owned vehicle

New Mexico does not indicate the weight of a vehicle on the license plate. Beginning in January 1991 a new graphic plate was introduced. This style plate will completely replace all previous passenger and truck plates by July 1993.

Personalized plates are available through Motor Vehicle Division, Special Plate Section Joseph M. Montoya Bldg., Santa Fe 87503. From 1 - 7 characters are permitted. The zia, spaces, dashes and apostrophes count as characters. There is an annual $15 fee.

To trace the owner through a plate number, requests should be made to Motor Vehicle Div. in Santa Fe. The fee is $4.00 per record requested.

NEW YORK

STATE ROUTE MARKER
60

★ **WFAN 660** New York
★ **WOR 710** New York
★ **WABC 770** New York
★ **WGY 810** Schenectady
★ **WCBS 880** New York
★ **WHAM 1180** Rochester
★ **WWKB 1520** Buffalo
★ **WQXR 1560** New York

AM RADIO

ROCHESTER
BUFFALO
SCHENECTADY
NEW YORK

NEW YORK A2B 123

2 PLATES VALIDATED BY
STICKER ON DRIVERS' SIDE
OF WINDSHIELD

NEW YORK ABC 123

PASSENGER REGULAR

NEW YORK PIPER

PERSONALIZED

NEW YORK 123456

DISABLED

NEW YORK 88 1234 STATE

STATE OWNED VEHICLE
1ST DIGITS MODEL YEAR
OF VEHICLE

NEW YORK A12345 OFFICIAL

COUNTY OR MUNICPAL
OWNED VEHICLE

NEW YORK NY SENATE 12 S 91 OFFICIAL 92

STATE SENATE SMALL 'S' IS
SECOND SET OF PLATES

NEW YORK GA1234 COMMERICAL

COMMERCIAL VEHICLE

NEW YORK SP1234 SPEC-COMM

SPECIAL PURPOSE AND
CONSTRUCTION EQUIPMENT

NEW YORK 1234A TRAILER

FULL AND SEMI-TRAILER

NEW YORK 9123456 DEALER

DEALER

NEW YORK SURVIVORS OF THE SHIELD 1

SURVIVORS OF POLICE
KILLED IN THE LINE OF DUTY

NEW YORK 5678 BIRTH PLACE OF BASEBALL

BASEBALL FAN
(SPECIAL PLATE)

NEW YORK GOLD STAR MOTHER 1234

MOTHER OF PERSON
KILLED IN WAR

NEW YORK V A S 1234

VOLUNTEER AMBULANCE
SERVICE MEMBER

NEW YORK CORONER 2345

CORONER

The "Empire State" issues two fully-reflectorized license plates using several different numeric configurations. A windshield sticker is used for two year period validation. The Statue of Liberty can appear on the left, right or center.

Distinctive captions:

COMMERCIAL - Vehicle used in commerce
FARM - Farm vehicle with restricted highway use
GOLD STAR MOTHER - Survivor of war casualty
LIVERY - Passenger vehicle for hire (often a limousine).
OFFICIAL - Any government owned vehicle
TRACTOR - Power unit of a tractor trailer combination.

T&LC - Non medallion cabs and limousines in NY City.
TRAILER - All types of trailers including semi-trailers.
SCHOOL - Vehicle that belongs to a school system
SPEC-COMM - Special purpose equipment - construction etc.
SURVIVORS OF THE SHIELD - Family of police killed on duty.

Other captions found on New York plates:

AMBULANCE	COUNTY COURT	HISTORICAL	SUPREME COURT
AIR NATIONAL GUARD	COURT OF APPEALS	JEWISH WAR VTRN.	SURROGATE COURT
APPORTIONED	COURT OF CLAIMS	JSC APPELLATE DIV	TAXI
ARMY NATIONAL GUARD	CRIMINAL COURT	MEDICAL EXAMINER	TOW TRUCK
BOARD OF SUPERVSRS.	DEALER	NAVAL MILITIA	TRANSPORTER
BUS	DISABLED VETERAN	NY ASSEMBLY	U.S. CONGRESS
CONGR. MEDAL HNR.	DISTRICT ATTORNEY	NY SENATE	U.S. SENATE
CORONER	DISTRICT COURT	NYC COUNCIL	VAN POOL
COUNTY LEGISLATOR	ENVIRON. CONSERV.	PEARL HARBOR SURV.	VOITURE
CITY COURT	POLICE	PURPLE HEART	
CIVIL COURT	FAMILY COURT	SEMI-TRAILER	
COUNTY CLERK	FORMER POW	STATE GUARD	

Codes:

New York issues 3 - 4 numeric- 3 alpha character plates in several configurations to regular passenger vehicles. Passenger plates with 1 or 2 alpha and 4-5 numerics are issued by county clerk offices. New York does not designate the county of origin or weight of a vehicle on plates. The following combinations are reserved for special groups:

AL (1-100) - American Legion officer
AR- Registered architect
(1-9999) **DAV** (1-9999) - Disabled veteran
DCH (1-9999) - Chiropractor
(1-9999) **DDS** (1-9999) - Dr. Dental Surgery
DS (201-1000) - Dentist
DSP- Dept. of State Police
(1-9999) **DV** - Paralyzed war veteran
(1-9999) **DPM**- Podiatrist
ED (1-9999)- Educator
(1-9999) **EMT** -Emergency Medical Technician.
(1-9999) **EMPT** - Emt paramedic
(1-20) **ESSEX** - Essex County Board Spvsr.
JUS (1-9) - Judge U.S. Customs Court
(1-20) **LBA** - Lieut. Benevolent Assn.
LBA (1-20) - Former Board member LBA
LCA (1-50) - Legislative correspondent
(1-9999) **LRT**- Licensed Radiology Technician.
2LU (2-999) - Limited use automobile
MD (1-99999) - Medical doctor
(1-99) **METRO** (1-99) - Metropol. Police Conf.
NYP - New York Press
NCAP (1-999) - Nassau Cty. Aux. Police
NCPBA (1-99) - Nassau County PBA
NYSCP - N.Y. Chiefs of Police
(1-999) **OD** - Opthomologist dispenser

(1-9999) **PBA** (1-9999) - Police Ben. Assn.
PE (1-9999) - Professional engineer
PSY (1000-1999) - Psychologist
PT (1000-1999) - Physiotherapist
RCL (1-50) - Rockland Cnty Supervisor
(1-9999) **RLC** (1-9999) - Rural letter carrier
(1-9999) **RN** (901-9999) - Registered nurse
RPA (1-9999) - Registered Physician's Assnt.
(1-9999) **RX** (1-9999)- Pharmacist
SBA (1-20) - Sgt. Benevolent Assn.
SFF (1-120) - State Firefighter Assn.
(1-9999) **SMA** (1-9999)- State Magistrate
(1-999) **TV** (1-999) - Television crew
TWY- New York Thruway Authority
UFA (1-9999) - Uniformed Fire. Assn
UPI (1-9999) - United Press
USALJ - U.S. Admin. Law Judge
USJ - Federal Court Judge
VA (1000-9999) - Dealer issued comm.plate
VAA (100-999) - Dealer issue pass. plate
VAS (100-999) - Volunteer ambulance service
VF (1-99999) - Volunteer fireman
VM- Veterinarian
(1-9999) **VFW** (1-9999) - Veterans of Fgn. Wars
VN- Visiting nurse
ZAA-ZZZ (100-999) - Rental vehicle

Personalized plate applications are available at NY Motor Vehicle branches or County Clerk offices. The fee is $25 per year, up to 8 characters permitted.

To Trace a NY plate through Mtr. Veh. Dept, Registration Records Section, Empire State Mall, Albany 12228. Fee $2 per record request.

NORTH CAROLINA

STATE ROUTE MARKER

12

AM RADIO

EZA-1234
NORTH CAROLINA

1 PLATE VALIDATED
BY 2 DECALS

WINSTON-SALEM
RALEIGH
CHARLOTTE
FAYETTEVILLE

WFNC 640 Fayetteville
WPTF 680 Raleigh
WBT 1110 Charlotte
WSMX 1500 Winston-Salem

First in Flight
RHETT
NORTH CAROLINA

PERSONALIZED

First in Flight
HD1234
NORTH CAROLINA

HANDICAPPED

First in Flight
12345
NORTH CAROLINA

NORTH CAROLINA
STATE UNIVERSITY

First in Flight
U0000
NORTH CAROLINA

UNIVERSITY OF
NORTH CAROLINA

First in Flight
PH 1944
NORTH CAROLINA

PURPLE HEART
RECIPIENT

Medal of Honor
CMH 8
NORTH CAROLINA

MEDAL OF HONOR
RECIPIENT

First in Flight
4
NORTH CAROLINA

STATE OFFICIAL
NUMERICS 1-280

NORTH CAROLINA
NR 336
NAVAL RESERVE

NAVAL RESERVE

19 COMMERCIAL 93
BJ-9738
NORTH CAROLINA

COMMERCIAL TRUCK

NC COMMERCIAL 93
ZF-5338
FOR HIRE

FOR HIRE VEHICLE
ANNUAL PLATE

PEARL HARBOR SURVIVOR
001
NORTH CAROLINA

PEARL HARBOR SURVIVOR

NORTH CAROLINA
TX-3726
1993

TAXI

NORTH CAROLINA
ZA-1051
1993

DRIVE AWAY PLATE

NORTH CAROLINA
TP-2941
1993

TRANSPORTER

N.C. PERMANENT
PX1234

STATE OWNED
VEHICLE

NORTH CAROLINA

The "Tarheel State" issues one fully-reflectorized license plate. The last general re-issue was in 1980, so there are a number of older plates in use (some not reflectorized). Current plates are three alpha - four numeric while previous issues were three alpha- three numeric.

Distinctive captions:

FIRST IN FLIGHT- Commemorates Wright brothers flight at Kitty Hawk NC.
PERMANENT- Permanent plate issued to city and county owned vehicles.
HORSELESS CARRIAGE- Vehicle at least 50 years old.
ANTIQUE- Collector's vehicle between 35 - 49 years old.

Codes:

North Carolina issues 3 alpha - 4 numeric character plates to passenger vehicles. Trucks and other non-passenger vehicle plates have a 1 or 2 alpha prefix followed by numerics. Alpha prefix codes are as follows:

AAA - ZZZ	Regular passenger	**LA-LF**	Apportioned truck
AA - BF	Private truck 5000lbs & up	**M**	5 year trailer plate
A - E	Trailer	**ME**	Special mobil equipment
CAP	Civil Air Patrol	**MF**	Manufacturer
DA	Dist. Atty (Num. is district)	**NC**	National guard
DOT	Dept of Transportation	**P**	(prefix or suffix) Permanent
DV	Disabled veteran	**PX - PZ**	State owned
FA - FZ	Farm vehicle	**POW**	Former Prisoner of War
FD	Franchised auto dealer	**RA - RZ**	Rental car
HD	Handicapped driver	**RF**	Rescue fireman
HP	Highway Patrol	**RS**	Rescue
ID	Independent auto dealer	**TA**	Taxi
J	Judiciary (numeric is district)	**TA**	Transporter
	1-19 Supreme Court and Appeals Court	**US**	Federal Judge (low number
	21-99 Superior Court (district plus 20)		indicates seniority)
	101-199 District Court Judge (dist +100)	**VF**	Volunteer fireman
	Suffix A- Additional Judge in district	**ZA**	Drive away
	(Junior seniority)	**ZB - ZF**	Common carrier, contract
L	Apportioned trailer		carrier, bus for hire
1-280	State Officials		

North Carolina does not designate county of origin or weight of vehicle on plates.

Personalized plate applications are available by mail from Div. of Motor Vehicles, Raleigh 27697. Up to 8 alpha and/or numeric characters can be requested. The fee is $20 in addition to annual registration charge.

To trace the owner of a North Carolina registered vehicle, write to Div. of Motor Vehicles, 1100 New Bern Ave. Raleigh 27697. Give the plate number and request an abstract of the registration. The fee is $1.00 per inquiry.

NORTH DAKOTA

KCJB 910 Minot
KBMR 1130 Bismarck
KNOX 1310 Grands Forks
KTYN 1430 Minot

STATE
ROUTE MARKER

AM RADIO

2 PLATES VALIDATED
BY ONE DECAL
ON BOTH PLATES

PERSONALIZED

HANDICAPPED

STATE/CITY/COUNTY
OWNED VEHICLE

ELECTED STATE OFFICIALS
(1-6)

TRAILER

USED CAR DEALER

INTERSTATE TRAILER
PRORATED

INTERSTATE TRACTOR
PRORATED

NEW CAR DEALER

DEVILS LAKE SIOUX TRIBE
TRIBAL ISSUE

TURTLE MOUNTAIN
CHIPPEWA TRIBE
TRIBAL ISSUE

AMATEUR RADIO

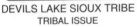

FORMER POW

COLLECTORS VEHICLE
40 YEARS OLD

DISABLED VETERAN

78

The "Peace Garden State" issues two fully-reflectorized license plates. Most passenger plates are issued in the three alpha - three numeric format, however low numbers 1 to 10,000 are also issued, as well as a new series prefixed ND.

Distinctive captions:
OFCL-State ,city, county owned vehicles
Peace Garden State- A park located on the Canadian border dedicated to peace.
Pioneer- Collectors vehicle 40 years old restored to its original condition.

Codes:
North Dakota issues 3 alpha-3 numeric character plates to regular passenger cars and trucks. These plates have no county or weight codes. Owners can request a specific number plate (Between 7 - 10,000) which will be issued at no extra charge if available.

Special class vehicles have an alpha prefix :

DV - Disabled Veteran
FR - Auto manufacturers rep.
E - State /city vehicle (tax exempt)
MH - Mobile home dealer
N - New car dealer
POW - Former prisoner of war
PR - Prorated vehicle

PT - Prorated trailer
SD - Semi-trailer dealer
J - Trailer
U - Used car dealer
DD - Dealer demonstrator
DX - Dealer in transit

Low numbers are issued to:

1. State Governor
2. Senior U.S. Senator
3. Junior U.S. Senator
4. U.S. Congressman

5. Governor's second vehicle
6. Lieutenant Governor
ND2 - Lt. Governor

Farm trucks can be distinguished by a red sticker on the plate.

Personalized plates are available for $25 per year from Vehicle Services Division 608 E. Boulevard, Bismarck, ND 58505. Up to 6 letters plus one space will be considered.

To trace the owner of a vehicle by the plate- complete "information request" form available at Vehicle Service Division. The fee is $3.00 for each inquiry.

OHIO

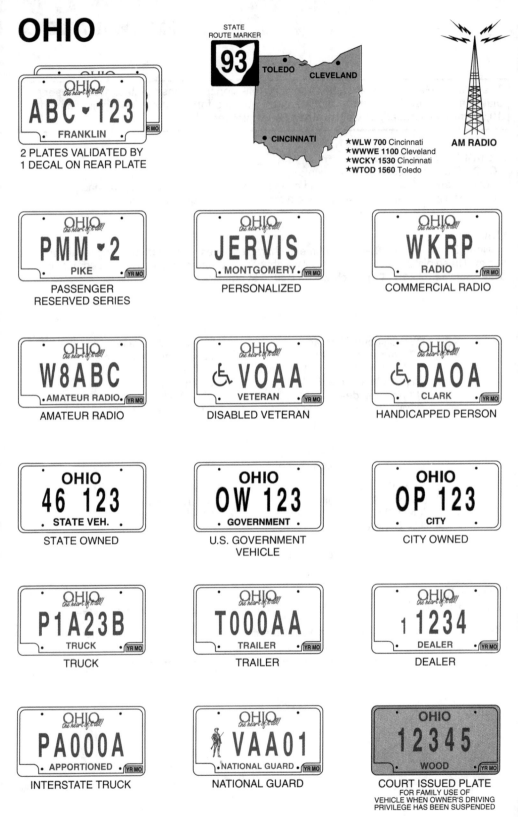

STATE ROUTE MARKER
93

TOLEDO
CLEVELAND
CINCINNATI

★WLW 700 Cincinnati
★WWWE 1100 Cleveland
★WCKY 1530 Cincinnati
★WTOD 1560 Toledo

AM RADIO

OHIO
the heart of it all!
ABC♥123
FRANKLIN
YR MO

2 PLATES VALIDATED BY
1 DECAL ON REAR PLATE

OHIO
the heart of it all!
PMM♥2
PIKE YR MO

PASSENGER
RESERVED SERIES

OHIO
the heart of it all!
JERVIS
MONTGOMERY YR MO

PERSONALIZED

OHIO
the heart of it all!
WKRP
RADIO YR MO

COMMERCIAL RADIO

OHIO
the heart of it all!
W8ABC
AMATEUR RADIO YR MO

AMATEUR RADIO

OHIO
the heart of it all!
♿VOAA
VETERAN YR MO

DISABLED VETERAN

OHIO
the heart of it all!
♿DAOA
CLARK YR MO

HANDICAPPED PERSON

OHIO
46 123
STATE VEH.

STATE OWNED

OHIO
OW 123
GOVERNMENT

U.S. GOVERNMENT
VEHICLE

OHIO
OP 123
CITY

CITY OWNED

OHIO
the heart of it all!
P1A23B
TRUCK YR MO

TRUCK

OHIO
the heart of it all!
TOOOAA
TRAILER YR MO

TRAILER

OHIO
the heart of it all!
1 1234
DEALER YR MO

DEALER

OHIO
the heart of it all!
PA000A
APPORTIONED YR MO

INTERSTATE TRUCK

OHIO
the heart of it all!
VAA01
NATIONAL GUARD YR MO

NATIONAL GUARD

OHIO
12345
WOOD YR MO

COURT ISSUED PLATE
FOR FAMILY USE OF
VEHICLE WHEN OWNER'S DRIVING
PRIVILEGE HAS BEEN SUSPENDED

OHIO

The "Buckeye State" issues two fully-reflectorized license plates. Passenger plates are required to display a county name decal.

Distinctive captions:

C.A.P -Civil Air Patrol
CS- Foreign Consular Service (Honorary)
FARM BUS - Bus used exclusively to transport farm workers
GOVERNMENT- Vehicle owned by the Federal Government
HISTORICAL - Collector's vehicle at least 25 years old. (Black on white)
IN TRANSIT - Used to transport new and used vehicles
HOUSE VEH - House car, house trailer or travel trailer
NON-COMM - 3/4 Ton or less capacity, non profit use
PURPLE HEART - Veteran who was wounded in combat.
RADIO- Owner of a commercial radio station
SPECIAL- Plate used to road test motor vehicles by a non motor vehicle dealer.
TELEVISION - Commercial TV station
VETERAN - Disabled veteran
SENIOR - Bus used by senior citizens

Codes:

Passenger car plates have 3 alpha- 3 numeric characters divided by an outline of the state.The county name appears on a sticker at the bottom of the plate. There are no codes on Ohio license plates.

Ohio has a special red on yellow plate that is issued by a court order to the family of a vehicle owner who has lost the privilege to drive. Known as a "Family Plate" it permits other members of the family to operate the vehicle during the term of the suspension.

Personalized license plate applications are available from Ohio Bureau of Motor vehicles, Reservations Section MVVPR, P.O.Box 16521, Columbus 43216 . Reserved series or any combination of 4 - 6 alpha permitted. Fee is $35 for personalized plates, $10 for reserved series plus normal registration charges.

To trace the owner of a vehicle write to: Bureau of Motor Vehicles, P.O.Box 16520 Columbus 43266-0020. Give them the plate number and request an abstract of the registration. The fee is $1.50 per record.

OKLAHOMA

STATE ROUTE MARKER

50

★ KVOO 1170 Tulsa
KRMG 740 Tulsa
KGYN 1210 Guymon
KOMA 1520 Oklahoma City

GUYMON • TULSA • OKLAHOMA CITY

AM RADIO

OKLAHOMA OK!
ABC 123
1 PLATE VALIDATED
2 DECALS

XHN - 52 **Oklahoma** is OK!
PASSENGER OLDER ISSUE
(SUNBELT BACKROUND)

OKLAHOMA
AD-1234
PASSENGER
OLDER ISSUE

OKLAHOMA OK!
DOKEY
PERSONALIZED CHOICE OF
BLUE, GREEN, GRAY, WHITE
CHAMOIS OR SAND BACKGROUND

OKLAHOMA OK!
HD 123 &
DISABLED

OKLAHOMA OK!
PAN123
PANHANDLE STATE
UNIVERSITY
PANHANDLE
STATE UNIVERSITY

OKLAHOMA IS OK!
1-4123
STATE
PUBLICLY OWNED VEHICLE
STATE/COUNTY OR OTHER
SUBDIVISION

ABSENTEE SHAWNEE TRIBE
LI·SI·WI·NI
000
Oklahoma
ABSENTEE SHAWNEE TRIBE
TRIBAL ISSUE

SAC & FOX NATION
SF 1000
OKLAHOMA
SAC & FOX NATION
FOR USE ON RESERVATION
TRIBAL ISSUE

OKLAHOMA OK!
TRB 123
TRIBAL VEH.
VEHICLE OWNED BY TRIBE
(OSAGE SYMBOL BACKROUND)

123 - 456T **Oklahoma** is OK!
COMMERCIAL TRUCK

OKLAHOMA
PHA 000
PURPLE HEART
PURPLE HEART RECIPIENT

OKLAHOMA OK!
12345
ARMY RESERVE
MILITARY RESERVE

OKLAHOMA OK!
PEARL HARBOR SURVIVOR 123
PEARL HARBOR 1941-1991
PEARL HARBOR
SURVIVOR

OKLAHOMA
NATIONAL GUARD
MVNON
ACTIVE & RETIRED
GUARD MEMBERS

OKLAHOMA
12 POW
PURPLE HEART
FORMER PRISONER
OF WAR

82

The "Sooner State" issues one fully-reflectorized license plate. Oklahoma has not had a general plate re-issue since 1979 and there are three different bases currently in use. The first letters on the passenger plate are a county code.

Distinctive captions:
ANTIQUE- Vehicle 30 years or older used for exhibition.
CLASSIC- Collector vehicle plate - replaces Antique **D.A.V -** Disabled American Veteran
E - Tax exempt
INTRANSIT- Vehicle hauling for hire (i.e. prefab houses)
TRIBAL VEH. - Vehicle owned by Indian tribe

Codes:
Oklahoma issues 3 alpha -3 numeric plates to passenger vehicles. Older plates still in use during 1991 have a 2 alpha county code prefix:

AD - Adair(Stillwell)
AL - Alfalfa(Cherokee)
AT - Atoka(Atoka)
BV - Beaver(Beaver City)
BK, BE - Beckham(Sayre)
BL - Blaine(Watonga)
BR, CY - Bryan(Durant)
CA, CD - Caddo(Anadarko)
CN, CNN, CX, CXX, CNN- Canadian (El Reno)
CR, CRR, CE - Carter (Ardmore)
CZ, CZZ - Cherokee
CW - Choctaw (Hugo)
CI - Cimmaron (Boise city)
CL, CLL, CV, CY, CF, CYY
CVV - Cleveland(Norman)
CO - Coal (Colgate)
CB, CC, CH, CM, CP, CCB - Commanche (Lawton)
CT - Cotton (Walters)
CG - Graf (Vinitia)
CJ, CK, CKK - Creek

CS, CSS,CZ -Custer (Arapaho)
DL, DE - Delaware (Jay)
DW - Dewey(Taloga)
EL - Ellis (Armatt)
GA, CR, GF, GB - Garfield
GN, GV- Garvin (Pauls Vly)
GD, CY- Grady (Chksha.)
GT - Grant (Medford)
GE - Greer (Mangum)
HM - Haron (Hollis)
HP - Harper (Buffalo)
HK - Haskell (Stigler)
HG - Hughes (Holdenville)
JA, JK, JS, JX - Jackson
JE - Jefferson (Wavaika)
JN - Johnson (Tishomingo)
KA, KK,KY ,KAY- Newkirk
KF - Kingfisher (Kingfisher)
HW - Kiowa (Hobart)
LA - Latimer (Wilburton)
LE, LF - LeFlore (Poteau)
LN, LL - Lincoln (Chandler)
LG, LO - Logan (Guthrie)

LV - Love (Marietta)
ML, MN - McClain (Purcell)
MC, MT- McCurtainl
MO - McIntosh (Eufaula) MA - Major (Fairview)
MR - Marshall (Madill)
ME,MY - Mayes (Pryor)
MU - Murray (Sulphur)
MG, MK, MS, MB - Muskoge
NB - Noble (Perry)
NW - Nowata (Nowata)
OK - Okfuskee (Okemah)
OL,OM - Okmulgee
OA, OE, OG, OS - Osage
OT, OW - Ottawa (Miami)
PW - Pawnee (Pawnee)
PA, PY, PF - Payne
PB, PS - Pittsburg
PC, PN - Pontotoc (Ada)
PE, PT, PD, PTT- Pottawatomie (Shawnee)
PM - Pushmataha (Antlers)
RM - Roger Mills (Cheynn.)

RG, RE, RO - Rogers
SE, SM - Seminole
SY, SH - Stephens(Duncn)
TX, TS - Texas(Guymon)
TL - Tillman(Frederick)
WG, WN - Wagoner
WA, WH, WS, WI - Washington(Bartlesville)
WT - Washita (Cordell)
WD -Woods (Alva)
WW, WE - Woodward
XA - XZ (except I & Q) - Oklahoma City (Okla Cty)
YA - YS (except I) - Okla. (Okla. City)
ZA - ZZ (except I&Q)Tulsa
ZZA - ZZG - Tulsa (Tulsa)

Other codes:
D - Dealer
KIA - Unremarried spouse of person killed in action
H- Okla. House of Rep.

POW - Former prisoner war
S - Oklahoma Senate
T- Commercial truck
V - Motor home

Oklahoma does not designate the weight of a vehicle on the license plate.

Personalized plates (are available in 6 different color combinations) - application forms available from Oklahoma Tax Commission, Motor Vehicle Dept., 2501 Lincoln Blvd., Oklahoma City,73194. 1 to 7 alpha/numeric characters permitted. Fee $12. Collegiate plates for each of the 26 state supported colleges available for extra $25 fee.

To trace the owner of an Oklahoma registered vehicle, write to Oklahoma Tax Commission, Motor Vehicle Div, 2501 Lincoln Blvd, Oklahoma City 73194. Give them the plate number and request an abstract of the registration. There is a $1.00 fee per record request.

OREGON

STATE ROUTE MARKER

99

★ **KEX 1190** Portland
KXL 750 Portland
KAGO 1150 Klamath Falls
KDUK 1280 Eugene

AM RADIO

RBC 123

2 PLATES VALIDATED
FOR A 2 YEAR PERIOD BY
2 DECALS ON BOTH PLATES

ABC123

PASSENGER OLDER
PLATE STILL IN USE
(ALSO GOLD ON BLUE PLATES)

QBC 123

PASSENGER
OLDER ISSUE

TIMBER

PERSONALIZED

D 00589

DISABLED VETERAN

T4111381

TRUCK

TR123 A

TRANSPORTER

E112345

GOVERNMENT
OWNED VEHICLE

DA 1665A

DEALER

CONSULAR CORPS
OFFICIAL 55

FOREIGN CONSUL
(HONORARY POSITION)

STATE REP 45

ELECTED OFFICIAL

F123456

FARM

NG 12345

NATIONAL GUARD

CN 00001

CHARITABLE ORGANIZATION

KA7PRF

AMATEUR RADIO

ANTIQUE VEHICLE
AQ 02348

CAR MUST BE 1/2 THE AGE
OF THE AUTO INDUSTRY
(1900-1992)-46 YRS

84

The "Pacific Wonderland" issues two fully-reflectorized license plates. Oregon has not had a general plate re-issue since 1955, and there are many different bases currently in use. Oregon registers motor vehicles for a two year period, and has the lowest registration fees in the nation.

Distinctive captions:
ANTIQUE VEHICLE: Collector's vehicle at least half the age of the auto industry which began 1900.

PERMANENT FLEET: Vehicle registered as part of a fleet.

PUBLICLY OWNED: State, city, county government owned vehicles (Includes Indian tribal govt owned vehicles.)

r

Codes:
Oregon issues 3 alpha - 3 numeric plates to passenger cars. There are no county of origin or other codes in the numbering system. Several older issue passenger plates with different color combinations are still valid for use.

All truck, trailer, bus and other non-passenger car plates have
an alpha prefix followed by numerics.
The prefix codes are as follows:

B	- Bus	**L over F**	- Light fixed load (under 3M)
C over N	- Charity/non profit trk, bus.	**L over T**	- Light trailer
D over A	- Oregon dealer	**P over W**	- Former Prisoner of War
E	- Publicly owned vehicle	**R**	-Travel trailer
F	-Farm vehicle	**S over P**	- Special interest vehicle
F over R	- For rent trailer		(25 years old)
H	- Motor home	**ST**	- Special use trailer
H over F	- Fixed load (over 3,000lbs)	**T**	-Truck
H over P	- Heavy trailer (permanent)	**T over W**	- Tow Truck
H over T	- Heavy trailer	**TR**	-Transporter
K	- Camper	**U**	- Light trailer

Oregon does not indicate the county or origin or weight of a vehicle on license plates.

Personalized plate applications are available at any field office of Motor Vehicles Div. A maximum of 6 alpha or numeric characters can be requested .Oregon registers vehicles for a 2 year period, therefore the cost for personalized plates is $50 in addition to the normal $30 regular fee.

To Trace the owner of an Oregon plate- write or visit Motor Veh. Div.,1905 Lana Ave. NE, Salem 97314. Fee is $4 per registration record request.

PENNSYLVANIA

KEYSTONE STATE
AAA·1234
MO/YR PENNSYLVANIA

1 PLATE VALIDATED
1 DECAL

STATE
ROUTE MARKER

39

★ KDKA 1020 Pittsburgh
WEEP 1080 Pittsburgh
★ KYW 1060 Philadelphia
★ WOGL 1210 Philadelphia
WPGR 1540 Philadelphia

PITTSBURGH

PHILADELPHIA

AM RADIO

PASSENGER OLDER ISSUE
(STILL IN USE)

RBC·123
MO/YR PENNSYLVANIA

PASSENGER OLDER ISSUE
(STILL IN USE)

PERSONALIZED

DV-12345
MO/YR PENNSYLVANIA

DISABLED VETERAN

KEYSTONE STATE
12345
MO/YR PENNSYLVANIA

DISABLED PERSON

OFFICIAL USE
PA-59899
MO/YR PENNSYLVANIA

STATE OWNED VEHICLE

MUNICIPAL OWNED
VEHICLE

TRUCK
67499-CE
MO/YR PENNSYLVANIA

COMMERCIAL TRUCK

FIRE DEPARTMENT

INTERSTATE TRUCK

VEHICLE USED
IN AGRICULTURE

PRESS
PHOTOGRAPHER

PENN STATE ALUMNI
COLLEGIATE PLATE

DUCKS UNLIMITED MEMBER

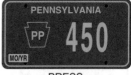

CONGRESSIONAL
MEDAL OF HONOR RECIPIENT
(INITIALS PREFIX)

The "Keystone State" issues one partially-reflectorized (glass beads on paint) license plate. Pennsylvania has not had a general plate re-issue since 1977 and there are three different bases in use.

Distinctive captions:

ANTIQUE - Collector's vehicle 25 years or older.
CLASSIC CAR - Exhibition vehicle 10 years or older- a discontinued model.
HEARING IMPAIRED - Driver with special limited hearing condition.
HUSBANDRY - Farm vehicle with limited highway use.
KEYSTONE STATE - Commemorates Pennsylvania's "keystone" position in the center of the original thirteen colonies.
STREET ROD - Modified exhibition vehicle built in 1948 or earlier.

- Press photographer   - State Senator   - Pa. House

Codes:

Regular passenger plates have 6 characters: All numeric, 3 alpha - 3 numeric, 1 alpha -5 numeric (alpha rotates and can be found in all positions)

The following alpha and numeric combinations are reserved for special use:

1, 2	- Governor and Lt. Gov.	**HP**	- Handicapped person
3 - 23	- Governor's cabinet.	**MG** (prefix or suffix)	- Mun. Govt.
24 - 999	- State officials and dignitaries	**PA** (10000 - 99999)	- State owned.
		PA (1-50)	- PA. Senate
DV	- Disabled veteran	**PA** (51-99)	- PA. Senate retired
EV	- Emergency vehicle	**PP**	- Press photographer
FF	- Firefighter	**USC** (1-25)	- U.S Congress
FD	- Fire Department	**USS** (1-4)	- U.S. Senate
HR (1 - 203)	- PA . House of Representatives.		

Dealer plates have 7 characters and the Alpha suffix indicates the type:
A - New car   **B** - Used car   **C** - MV business **D,E,F**- All types of dealers

Commercial vehicle, tractor, taxi, bus and trailer plates have 7 characters and the following alpha prefixes indicate the class of vehicle:

AA - AZ - Apportioned truck
BA - Bus
HC - HD - Motor home
IMP - Implement of husbandry (farm)
LM- Limousine
M over T - Mass transit

R - Reposessor
SA - SB - School bus
SME - Special mobile equipment
TA - TZ - Trailer
TX - Taxi
YA - YZ, CA - CZ (suffix or prefix) - Truck

Pennsylvania does not indicate county of origin or weight of a vehicle on plates.

Pennsylvania issues personalized and many special and college plates. Applications are available from Notary Publics, university alumni office and / or PA Dept of Transportation . The central office is in Harrisburg 17122. Up to 7 alpha numeric characters are allowed. The initial fee is $20 ; yearly renewal $24.

To Trace the owner through a plate number, write to Commonwealth of PA Bureau of Driver Licensing, Harrisburg 17122. Fee $5 per record requested.

RHODE ISLAND

WPRO **630** Providence
WALE **990** Providence
WHIM **1110** Providence

PROVIDENCE

STATE ROUTE MARKER

R.I. **10**

BLOCK ISLAND

AM RADIO

⊥ OCEAN STATE
ZK-123
RHODE ISLAND MO-YR

2 PLATES VALIDATED
EVERY 2 YEARS BY 1
DECAL ON BOTH PLATES

⊥ OCEAN STATE
1234
RHODE ISLAND MO-YR

PASSENGER

RHODE ISLAND
AB 23
Ocean State MO-YR

OPTIONAL PLATE
AVAILABLE
FOR EXTRA FEE

⊥ OCEAN STATE
FERGUS
RHODE ISLAND MO-YR

PERSONALIZED

⊥ VETERAN
123
RHODE ISLAND MO-YR

DISABLED VETERAN

⊥ PUBLIC
1234
RHODE ISLAND MO-YR

FOR HIRE VEHICLE

RHODE ISLAND
1234
STATE MO-YR

STATE OWNED

OCEAN STATE
POLICE **123**
RHODE ISLAND

POLICE

⊥ OCEAN STATE
C O M M **12345**
RHODE ISLAND MO-YR

COMMERCIAL

⊥ TRAILER
12345
RHODE ISLAND MO-YR

TRAILER

⊥ FARM
1234
RHODE ISLAND MO-YR

FARM VEHICLE

JITNEY MO-YR
1234
RHODE ISLAND 68

BUS

⊥ BAILEE 91
1234
RHODE ISLAND MO-YR

REPOSSESSOR
COLORS CHANGE YEARLY

⊥ ANTIQUE
1234
RHODE ISLAND MO-YR

ANTIQUE CAR

⊥ COMBAT WOUNDED
200
RHODE ISLAND MO-YR

VETERAN WOUNDED
IN COMBAT

WAR VETERAN
P 8
RHODE ISLAND MO-YR

WAR VETERAN

RHODE ISLAND

The "Ocean State" state issues two fully-reflectorized license plates. Rhode Island passenger plates are all numeric, or one or two alpha followed by numerics. Plates are re-validated for two year periods.

Distinctive captions:
ANTIQUE: Collector's vehicle 25 years or older.
BAILEE: Repossessor **CITY**- City owned vehicle.
COMM - Commercial vehicle (truck).
FARM - Farm vehicle with limited highway use.
JITNEY - Bus plate (last manufactured in 1968) but still in use.
MOTOR VEHICLE REGISTRY - Plates issued to the Registrar of Motor Vehicles , his deputies and inspectors.
NEWS PHOTOG - News photographer accredited in Rhode Island.
PUBLIC - Motor vehicle for hire.
STATE - State owned vehicle.
SUB - Station wagons (old plate but some still in use).
TOWN - Vehicle owned by a town.
VETERAN - Disabled veteran.
HANDICAPPED PARKING PLACARD - The wheelchair symbol is used. Placard can be transferred to any vehicle used by the disabled person.

Codes:
Rhode Island passenger car plates are all numeric (1-99999) or 1-2 alpha followed by 1-3 numeric (A-1 through AA-123). Registrations are for a two year period. The only other type vehicles issued passenger type plates are vans with windows all around and passenger seating (not cargo vans). Pickup trucks receive commercial plates. Passenger plates are renewed on a schedule which corresponds to the first letter of the owners last name.

Trucks and other commercial vehicle plates are all numeric and clearly captioned. Rhode Island does not issue apportioned, tractor or handicapped license plates.

There are no county of origin , weight or use codes on Rhode Island plates. The majority of plates are issued for multi-year use. Dealers, bailee and transporter plates are replaced annually with a different color scheme

Personalized plate application forms are available from Registry of Motor Vehicles, State Office Bldg, Providence 02903. The personalized plate fee is an additional $30 per year, and the regular registration annual fee is $30. As a result of the 2 year registration system the renewal fee is $120 every 2 years.

To trace the owner of a Rhode Island vehicle, write to Registry of Motor Vehicles, State Office Bldg., Providence 02903. Send the plate number and request an abstract of the registration. The fee is $5 per request.

SOUTH CAROLINA

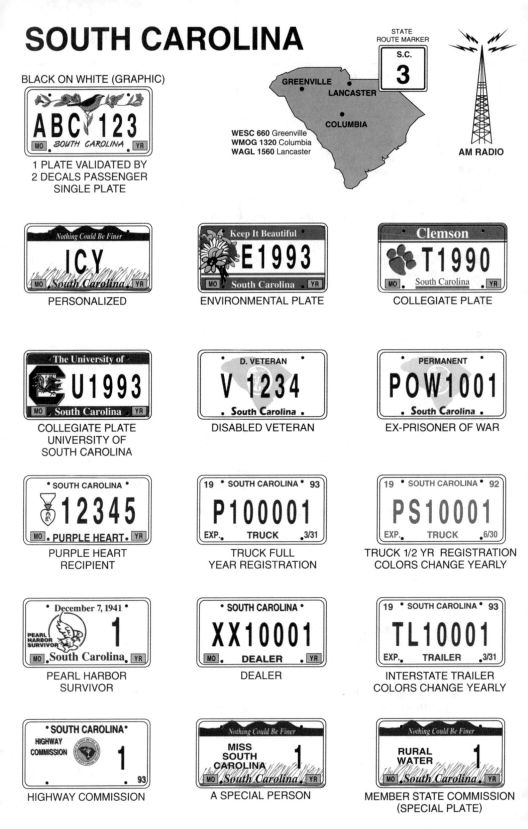

BLACK ON WHITE (GRAPHIC)

ABC 123
MO SOUTH CAROLINA YR

1 PLATE VALIDATED BY
2 DECALS PASSENGER
SINGLE PLATE

STATE
ROUTE MARKER
S.C.
3

WESC 660 Greenville
WMOG 1320 Columbia
WAGL 1560 Lancaster

AM RADIO

Nothing Could Be Finer
ICY
MO South Carolina YR

PERSONALIZED

Keep It Beautiful
E1993
MO South Carolina YR

ENVIRONMENTAL PLATE

Clemson
T1990
MO South Carolina YR

COLLEGIATE PLATE

The University of
U1993
MO South Carolina YR

COLLEGIATE PLATE
UNIVERSITY OF
SOUTH CAROLINA

D. VETERAN
V 1234
South Carolina

DISABLED VETERAN

PERMANENT
POW1001
South Carolina

EX-PRISONER OF WAR

SOUTH CAROLINA
12345
MO PURPLE HEART YR

PURPLE HEART
RECIPIENT

19 SOUTH CAROLINA 93
P100001
EXP. TRUCK 3/31

TRUCK FULL
YEAR REGISTRATION

19 SOUTH CAROLINA 92
PS10001
EXP. TRUCK 6/30

TRUCK 1/2 YR REGISTRATION
COLORS CHANGE YEARLY

December 7, 1941
1
PEARL HARBOR SURVIVOR
MO South Carolina YR

PEARL HARBOR
SURVIVOR

SOUTH CAROLINA
XX10001
MO DEALER YR

DEALER

19 SOUTH CAROLINA 93
TL10001
EXP. TRAILER 3/31

INTERSTATE TRAILER
COLORS CHANGE YEARLY

SOUTH CAROLINA
HIGHWAY COMMISSION 1
93

HIGHWAY COMMISSION

Nothing Could Be Finer
MISS SOUTH CAROLINA 1
MO South Carolina YR

A SPECIAL PERSON

Nothing Could Be Finer
RURAL WATER 1
MO South Carolina YR

MEMBER STATE COMMISSION
(SPECIAL PLATE)

The "Palmetto State" issues one fully-reflectorized license plate. It issues the second greatest (next to Illinois) variety of plates. Personalized and other special interest plates have a graphic design different from regular passenger.

Distinctive captions:

ANTIQUE AUTO - Collector's vehicle 30 years or older.
EMT - Emergency medical technician.
FARM - Vehicle used exclusively for farm and related industry.
M/R DEALER - Manufacturer's repossession plate.
RESCUE - Rescue vehicle.
U.S. MIL. RES - Member of active military reserve unit.
UTILITY - Utility trailer
WHOLESALER - Wholesale automobile dealer. (all of the above listed plates are renewed by a decal each yr. except-Antique)

Codes:

South Carolina issues 3 alpha - 3 numeric graphic design plates to private passenger, light trucks for multi-year use.

Personalized plates have a different graphic design than the regular passenger. This personalized design is used for 138 different special group plates such as: State Officials, educators, board members, and Miss South Carolina. These special plates, similar to personalized,are re-validated annually by decals.

State,city, county and municipal government plates are permanent and these also have a graphic background design of the state seal.

The prefixes on this plate design have special meaning :

CG	County Government	RG	Regional Government
MG	Municipal Government	SG	State Government
POW	Ex Prisoner of War	V	Disabled veteran

State government executives have special plates. The numbers are:

1. Governor	4. Treasurer	7. Dept of Education
2. Lt. Governor	5. Comptroller General	8. Adjutant General
3. Sec. of State	6. Attorney General	9. Dept. of Agriculture

Trucks are issued new non-graphic plates each year.Other commercial vehicle plates are re-validated by decal. These plates have a 1 or 2 alpha prefix followed by numerics. The following alpha prefixes have special meaning:

CC (suffix) - Common Carrier	SM - Special mobile equip
HT - House trailer	XX - Dealer
P - Truck	WX - Wholesale dealer
PS - Semi annual truck registration	

South Carolina does not indicate the county of origin on plates.

Personalized Plate applications are available from S.C. Dept of Highways and Transportation, P.O.Box 1498, Columbia 29216. 2 - 7 character alpha numeric combination will be considered. Fee $15 per year plus normal registration cost.

To trace the owner of a vehicle through the plate number, write to Division of Motor Vehicles in Columbia (see above) .Give the number and exact reason for asking .The fee is $2 per record requested.

SOUTH DAKOTA

2 PLATES VALIDATED
BY 1 DECAL
ON BOTH PLATES

STATE
ROUTE MARKER

34

KIMM 1150 Rapid City
KELO 1320 Sioux Falls
KKAA 1560 Aberdeen

ABERDEEN

RAPID CITY

SIOUX FALLS

AM RADIO

PERSONALIZED

HANDICAPPED

PEARL HARBOR SURVIVOR

STATE OWNED

COUNTY OWNED

CITY OWNED

CROW CREEK SIOUX
INDIAN TRIBE

LOWER BRULE SIOUX
INDIAN TRIBE

STANDING ROCK SIOUX
INDIAN TRIBE

DISABLED VETERAN

COMMERCIAL

MASS TRANSPORTATION
PERMANENT PLATE

FORMER PRISONER
OF WAR

NATIONAL GUARD

FIREFIGHTER

The "Home of Mount Rushmore" issues two fully reflectorized plates. The prefix on each passenger plate is a county code. New graphic plates with green numbers will replace the previous issue plates during 1991.

Distinctive captions:

CONSTR - Construction equipment
HISTORICAL- Collector's vehicle at least 30 years old.
TAX EXEMPT - State,county,city, non profit training centers, school and tribal vehicles.
GREAT FACES - Promotion for Mount Rushmore monument.

Codes:

South Dakota passenger plates have 6 characters. An older issue has a 3 alpha - 3 numeric design with a county code on a sticker. A new issue (to be used until 1995) has a 1 or 2 numeric prefix that is a county code. The code and county (county seats) are as follows:

1. Minnehaha (Sioux Falls)
2. Pennington (Rapid City)
3. Brown (Aberdeen)
4. Beadle (Huron)
5. Codington (Watertown)
6. Brookings (Brookings)
7. Yankton (Yankton)
8. Davison (Mitchell)
9. Lawrence (Deadwood)
10. Aurora (Plankinton)
11. Bennett (Martin)
12. Bon Homme (Tyndall)
13. Brule (Chamberlain)
14. Buffalo (Gannvalley)
15. Butte (Belle Fourche)
16. Campbell (Mound City)
17. Charles Mix(Lk.Andres)
18. Clark (Clark)
19. Clay (Vermillion)
20. Corson (McIntosh)
21. Custer (Custer)
22. Day (Webster)
23. Duel (Clear Lake)
24. Dewey (Timber Lake)

25. Douglas (Armour)
26. Edmunds (Ipswich)
27. Fall River (Hot Springs)
28. Faulk (Faulkton)
29. Grant (Milbank)
30. Gregory (Burke)
31. Haakon (Philip)
32. Hamlin (Hayti)
33. Hand (Miller)
34. Hanson (Alexandria)
35. Harding (Buffalo)
36. Hughes (Pierre)
37. Hutchinson (Olivet)
38. Hyde (Highmore)
39. Jackson (Kadoka)
40. Jerauld (Wessington Sprgs.)
41. Jones (Murdo)
42. Kingsbury (De Smet)
43. Lake (Madison)
44. Lincoln (Clinton)
45. Lyman (Kennebec)
46. McCook (Salem)
47. McPherson (Leola)
48. Marshall (Britton)

49. Meade (Sturgis)
50. Mellette (White River)
51. Miner (Howard)
52. Moody (Flandreau)
53. Perkins (Bison)
54. Potter (Gettysburg)
55. Roberts (Sisseton)
56. Sanborn (Mitchell)
57. Spink (Redfield)
58. Stanley (Fort Pierre)
59. Sully (Onida)
60. Tripp (Winner)
61. Turner (Parker)
62. Union (Elk Point)
63. Walworth (Selby)
64. Ziebach (Dupree)
65. Shannon (*Wounded Knee)
66. Yankton (Yankton)
67. Todd (*Antelope)
* Largest town
65,67 Are entirely within
     native American reservations
77. Dealer plate

Commercial vehicles are issued multi-year plates that do not have a graphic design. The characters are 1 alpha -4 numeric and the year and ton weight class appears on the validation sticker.

South Dakota Tax exempt plates are issued to state, city, county and tribal owned vehicles.

The following alpha prefix codes are used:

CCT - Crow Creek
CO - County owned
CRT - Cheyenne Riv. Tribe
CY - City owned
FST - Flandreau Sioux

GFP - Game, Fish,Park Dpt
HP - Highway Patrol
SC, ED - School vehicles
DE - Drivers education
LBT - Lower Brule Tribe

OST - Ogalalla Sioux Tribe
RST - Rosebud Sioux Tribe
SRT - Standing Rock Tribe
SWT - Sisseton-Wahpeton
YST - Yankton Sioux Tribe

Personalized plate application from Dept of Revenue, Mtr. Veh Div.,118 W.Capital Ave. Pierre, 57501. 2 - 6 alpha numeric characters allowed. Initial fee is $75, yearly renewal costs $10. Graphic Indian tribal design plates available to all residents at regular fee + $10.

To trace the owner of a South Dakota plate write to DMV 118 Capital Ave, Pierre 57501.Give them the plate number and the reason for the request. The fee is $2 per record; $5 for certified copies.

TENNESSEE

STATE ROUTE MARKER
76

★ WSM 650 Nashville
★ WLAC 1510 Nashville
WNOO 1260 Chattanooga
WHJM 1180 Knoxville

AM RADIO

1 PLATE VALIDATED 2 DECALS
AND WHEEL TAX DECAL
IN SOME COUNTIES & CITIES

SAMPLE PLATE
AVAILABLE FROM STATE

PERSONALIZED

HANDICAPPED

DISABLED VETERAN

STATE SENATE

STATE VEHICLE

POLICE/FIRE/AMBULANCE
CITY BUS

FOR HIRE TRUCK

SEMI-TRAILER

INTERSTATE TRUCK

EMERGENCY
VOL FIRE, AUX POL.,
C.A.P., CIVIL DEFENSE, ETC.

UNIVERSITY OF TENN.
COLLEGIATE PLATE

CONGRESSIONAL
MEDAL OF HONOR
RECIPIENT

PEARL HARBOR SURVIVOR

FORMER PRISONER
OF WAR

The "Volunteer State" issues one fully-reflectorized license plate. The county of origin appears on a decal at the bottom of each passenger plate. Personalized plates are made on a non-graphic format.

Distinctive captions:
ANTIQUE - Vehicle at least 25 years old.
EMERGENCY- Emergency services- including ham radio.
GOV'T SERVICE - Government owned vehicle.
JOINT - Plate issued to both farm and semi-commercial veh.

Codes:
Private passenger vehicle plates are 3 alpha - 3 numeric and the county name appears on the plate. Some counties have a wheel tax, and a decal on the lower right indicates payment.

Annual plates are issued to special classes of passenger cars. Most plates are clearly captioned, and the following can be recognized by the alpha prefix code:

GA - GZ - City,county govt veh.		**TX**	- Taxi
MUS - Music city (private bus owned by an entertainer)		**USJ**	- Federal Judge
		1	- Governor
S - State govt. vehicle.		**1X**	- Former governor

Trucks and other commercial vehicles are issued plates with a 2 alpha prefix code. Up until 1989 they were issued new plates yearly, currently they are revalidated by decal. The first alpha indicates class, the second is a weight code. Each class has its own second alpha weight code:

First alpha

P	- Private
H	- For Hire
M	- Moving van (Household)
S	- Joint (Semi comm- farm)
WD	- Well drill
FL	- Fixed load
BA	- Bus unlimited operation
BB - BD	- Bus limited area

Second alpha (Maximum Gross Wgt)
This is the weight code for Private trucks

A - BZ	9,000 lbs
M - MZ	16,000
P - PZ	20,000
R - RZ	26,000
S	32,000
T	38,000
U	44,000
V	56,000
W	66,000
X	74,000
Y	80,000

Semi-trailer plates are 1 alpha - 5 numeric. An alpha suffix is on apportioned .

Personalized plate applications must be made to Title and Registration Section, Audit Unit, Andrew Jackson State Office Bldg. Nashville 37242. Any combination of 3 - 7 characters will be considered. Fee $25 per yr. in addition to regular registration.

To trace the owner through a plate number write or phone : County clerk's office or Motor Vehicle Information Unit, Andrew Jackson Bldg, Nashville 37242. Give the plate number and request an abstract of the registration. The fee is $ 2.

TEXAS

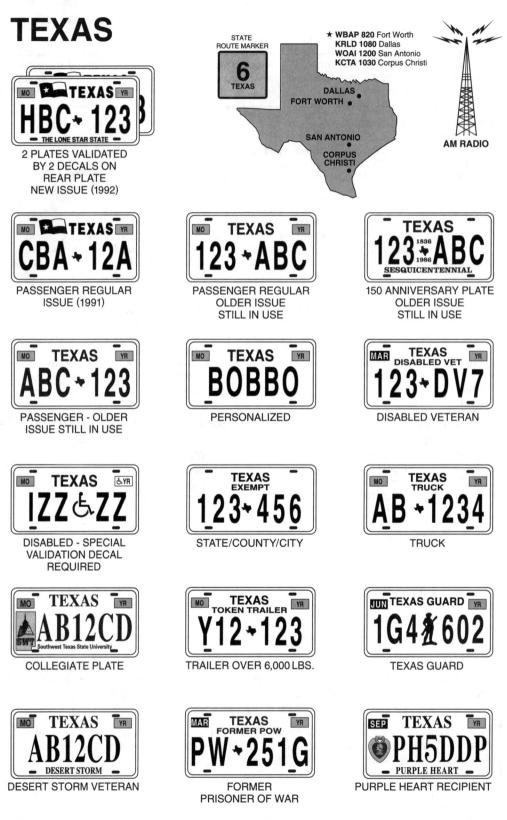

STATE ROUTE MARKER

6 TEXAS

★ **WBAP 820** Fort Worth
KRLD 1080 Dallas
WOAI 1200 San Antonio
KCTA 1030 Corpus Christi

DALLAS
FORT WORTH
SAN ANTONIO
CORPUS CHRISTI

AM RADIO

MO TEXAS **YR**
HBC-123
THE LONE STAR STATE

2 PLATES VALIDATED
BY 2 DECALS ON
REAR PLATE
NEW ISSUE (1992)

MO TEXAS **YR**
CBA-12A

PASSENGER REGULAR
ISSUE (1991)

MO TEXAS **YR**
123-ABC

PASSENGER REGULAR
OLDER ISSUE
STILL IN USE

TEXAS
123 1836 1986 ABC
SESQUICENTENNIAL

150 ANNIVERSARY PLATE
OLDER ISSUE
STILL IN USE

MO TEXAS **YR**
ABC-123

PASSENGER - OLDER
ISSUE STILL IN USE

MO TEXAS **YR**
BOBBO

PERSONALIZED

MAR TEXAS
DISABLED VET **YR**
123-DV7

DISABLED VETERAN

MO TEXAS **♿YR**
IZZ♿ZZ

DISABLED - SPECIAL
VALIDATION DECAL
REQUIRED

TEXAS
EXEMPT
123-456

STATE/COUNTY/CITY

MO TEXAS
TRUCK **YR**
AB-1234

TRUCK

MO TEXAS **YR**
AB12CD
SWT Southwest Texas State University

COLLEGIATE PLATE

MO TEXAS
TOKEN TRAILER **YR**
Y12-123

TRAILER OVER 6,000 LBS.

JUN TEXAS GUARD **YR**
1G4♟602

TEXAS GUARD

MO TEXAS **YR**
AB12CD
DESERT STORM

DESERT STORM VETERAN

MAR TEXAS
FORMER POW **YR**
PW-251G

FORMER
PRISONER OF WAR

SEP TEXAS **YR**
PH5DDP
PURPLE HEART

PURPLE HEART RECIPIENT

The "Lone Star State" issues two fully-reflectorized plates. Texas has not had a general re-issue since 1975 and there are six different bases in use.

Distinctive captions:

ANTIQUE - Collector's vehicle at least 25 years old.
COMBINATION - Truck or tractor over 1 ton in combination witha semi-trailer over 6000 lbs
CONSULAR OFFICIAL - Honorary position representing foreign government
CONSERVATION- Soil conservation equipment
DISASTER - Disaster relief vehicle operated by non profit organization.
EXEMPT- State or municipal owned vehicle.
MACHINERY - Water drilling or construction equipment.
PERMIT - Oil well equipment for highway use.
TEST CAR - Plate used by manufacturers to test new vehicles.
TOKEN TRAILER - Semi-trailer over 6,000 lbs pulled by tractor with a
combination plate.
TEXAS GUARD- Texas Air, State and National Guard.

Codes:

Regular passenger plates are 3 numeric - 3 alpha, and 3 aplha-2 numeric -1 alpha. Texas does not use county of origin or weight codes.

The county or origin can be traced by the small 6 - digit serial number printed on the validation stickers which are issued annually by the tax collectors in each of the 254 Texas counties. Truck, trailer, commercial plates have 6 characters with various alpha numeric combinations. Some examples are:

Prefix

Apportioned trailer	**12R - 59R**
Apportioned truck	**R**
Combination	**2AA - 2ZZ**
Farm truck	**1AA - 1ZZ , A1A - Z1Z** 100 - 999
Tractor	**T** (30 - 39,60 - 79)
Trailer	**A- H, J - N,Q, A - H, J, L- N**
Truck *	**AA -VF, VG-ZZ** 100-9999
	*Combinations omitted
	(DV, TT,VD,TX,XA-XZ)

Texas issues over 700,000 special license plates in 35 categories.

Amateur radio - 12,716	Exempt - 536,465	Purple Heart - 12,852	U.S.House of Rep. - 54
Antique -13,900	Fertilizer truck - 1,131	Soil Conservation - 545	U.S. Senate - 4
Civil Air Patrol - 15	Former POW - 3,500	State Capital - 63	U.S.Judge - 140
Classic - 929	Honorary Consul - 58	State Judge - 1,670	U.S.Marine Corps - 8
Collegiate - 7,963	Log Loader - 26	State Official - 452	U.S. Navy -28
Cong. Medal of Honor -14	Manufacturer - 158	Texas Guard - 1,985	Viet Nam Veteran - 410
Dealer - 52,000	Parade - 3	U.S Air Force -86	Vol. Firefighter - 2,638
Disabled Person - 216,477	Pearl Harbor Srvr. -1,070	U.S.Military Reserves -350	
Disabled Veteran - 28,099	Permit - 1,946	U.S.Army - 46	
Disaster Relief - 75	Personalized - 55,282	U.S.Coast Guard - 6	

Personalized plates form 35-A available from Motor Vehicle Div.40th & Jackson ,Austin 78779-0001 -6 alpha numeric characters. Fee $40 plus normal registration costs.

To trace a vehicle write DMV (see above) send the vehicle identification number number and your request. The fee is $2 per inquiry.

UTAH

2 PLATES VALIDATED BY 3
DECALS ON THE REAR PLATE
(COUNTY, MONTH, YEAR)

STATE
ROUTE MARKER

13

★ **KSL 1160** Salt Lake City
KFMY 960 Provo
KLGN 1390 Logan
KLO 1430 Ogden

LOGAN ●
OGDEN ●
SALT ●
LAKE CITY
● PROVO

AM RADIO

CENTENNIAL PLATE
ANNUAL 1992-1997

PASSENGER
OLDER ISSUE

PERSONALIZED

DISABLED PERSON

STATE SENATOR

COUNTY OR LOCAL
GOVT. VEHICLE

COMMERCIAL VEHICLE

TRAILER

DEALER

MANUFACTURER

NATIONAL GUARD

UTAH HIGHWAY PATROL

FORMER
PRISONER OF WAR

PEARL HARBOR SURVIVOR

COLLECTORS VEHICLE
30 YEARS OLD OR MORE
PERMANENT PLATE

UTAH

The "Beehive State" issues two fully-reflectorized plates. Utah has not had a general plate re-issue since 1973 and there are five different bases currently in use. A county decal (with a two letter abbreviation) is required to be displayed in the upper left corner of most plates.

Distinctive captions:
HORSELESS CARRIAGE : Vehicle at least 30 yrs old.
RADIO: F.C.C. licensed radio operator (Ham)

Codes:
Utah issues 3 numeric- 3 alpha character plates to private passenger vehicles. The numbering system is for individual vehicle identification only. County of origin appears on a 2 alpha decal applied to the upper left corner of the plate. The counties and (county seats) are as follows.

BV - Beaver (Beaver)
BE - Box Elder (Brigham City)
CA - Cache (Logan)
CC - Carbon (Price)
DG - Daggett (Manila)
DA - Davis (Farmington)
DU - Duchesne (Duchesne)
EM - Emery (Castle Dale)
GA - Garfield (Panguitch)
GR - Grand (Moab)
RN - Iron (Parowan)
JU - Juab (Nephi)
KA - Kane (Kanab)
MD - Millard (Fillmore)
MN - Morgan (Morgan)

PT - Piute (Junction)
RH - Rich (Randoph)
SL - Salt Lake (Salt Lake City)
SJ - San Juan (Monticello)
SP - Sanpete (Manti)
SE - Sevier (Richfield)
SU - Summit (Coalville)
TE - Tooele (Tooele)
UN - Uintah (Uintah)
UT - Utah (Utah)
WA - Wasatch (Wasatch)
WN - Washington (St. George)
WE - Wayne (Loa)
WB - Weber (Ogden)

Trucks,truck tractors, trailers, buses are issued multi-year (graphic base plates) with 1-3 alpha prefix or (suffix). The alpha codes are:

A - B,E Trailers over 750lbs unladen
D over L Dealer
FA - FB Farm vehicle

TN Transporter
MFG Manufacturer
WK Wrecker

Government owned vehicles have a prefix or (suffix) EX- meaning tax exempt.
Low numbers are issued to:
1- Governor, **EX2.**- Lt.Governor, **EX3** - State Treasurer, **EX4** - State Auditor

Utah does not designate the county or origin, weight class or use restrictions on commercial vehicle.plates.

Personalized plate applications are sent to Motor Vehicle Dept. 1095 Motor Ave., Salt Lake City 84116. 1 - 6 alpha/ numeric characters allowed. Initial fee is $30, and $5 thereafter in addition to regular registration fees.

To trace the owner of a Utah plate write to the Motor Vehicle Dept, 1095 Motor Ave, Salt Lake 84116. Give the plate number and ask for an abstract of the registration. The fee is $2 per inquiry.

VERMONT

ABC 123

2 PLATES VALIDATED
BY 1 DECAL BOTH PLATES

WVMT 620 Burlington
WSYB 1380 Rutland
WDOT 1390 Burlington

STATE
ROUTE MARKER

30

AM RADIO

VERMONT BICENTENNIAL

BICENTENNIAL PLATE

SYRUP

PERSONALIZED
UP TO 7 CHARACTERS

1234

HANDICAPPED

★ 567
SHERIFF

SHERIFF

WB1AJG

AMATEUR RADIO

MUN 1234

MUNICIPAL VEHICLE

AAB 123

TRUCK

AAE 123

TRAILER

11A01
APPORTIONED

INTERSTATE TRUCK
APPORTIONED

20T01

INTERSTATE TRAILER
(ONE PLATE)

A051

NEW CAR DEALER

12345

FIRE FIGHTERS
ASSOCIATION

73

LOW NUMBERS 1-99
ASSIGNED BY GOVERNOR

123VT

STATE OFFICIALS

12345

NATIONAL GUARD

The "Green Mountain State" issues two fully-reflectorized plates. All regular passenger plates issued since 1990 are three alpha- three numeric. Earlier configurations are still in use.

Distinctive captions:

ACD - Auction car dealer
AGR - Farm truck
ANTIQUE - Vehicle 25 years old..
ATV - All terrain vehicle (small plate)
CONTRACTOR - Contractor trailer.
EXHIBIT - Exhibition vehicle.
DLF - Farm machine dealer.
FCD - Finance car dealer.
DLH - Highway bldg.equip. dealer.

DLT - Trailer dealer
HUP - Truck highway use permit.
MUN - Municipal owned vehicle.
NCD - New car dealer
SPECIAL PURPOSE - Const. equip.
TRA - Trailer
TRK - Truck
UCD - Used car dealer
VOL- Volunteer fire company.

Codes:

Passenger car plates:
All regular passenger car plates issued since 1990 are 3 alpha - 3 numeric.
Earlier configurations still in use are :

all numeric (1-9999)
alpha - numeric format:
1A123
123A4
1AA23
12AA3
Alphas **I, J, O, QU, V, Z** are not used on Vermont plates

Low numbers (1-99) are assigned by the Governor's office.
100-999 **VT** are assigned to state board members and appointees. Plates are valid only for the term of office.
(Prefix) **DE** - Drivers education vehicle.

Trucks and commercial vehicles:
Various alpha numeric configurations are used. The vehicle class is designated by a caption or decal. Vermont does not designate the county of origin or the weight of a vehicle on license plates.

Personalized plate application forms are available from State of Vermont Dept of Motor Vehicles, 120 State St. Montpelier, 05603-0001. A maximum of 7 characters but only 2 numerics can be used. The fee is $20 per year in addition to the regular registration fee.

To trace the owner of a vehicle, write to: Dept of Motor Vehicles, Montpelier 05603. Give the plate number and request an abstract of the registration. The fee is $4 .

VIRGINIA

2 PLATES VALIDATED
WITH 2 DECALS
ON BOTH PLATES

STATE
ROUTE MARKER
7

★ **WRVA 1140** Richmond
WLVA 590 Lynchburg
WNIS 850 Norfolk
WKBA 1550 Roanoke

RICHMOND
LYNCHBURG
ROANOKE
NORFOLK

AM RADIO

PASSENGER, OPTIONAL
GREAT SEAL PLATE

PASSENGER, BICENTENNIAL
ALL NUMERIC OR PERSONALIZED

PURPLE HEART RECIPIENT

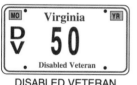

DISABLED VETERAN

ELECTED STATE OFFICIAL

STATE VEHICLE

LOCAL GOVT. VEHICLE

COMMERCIAL TRUCK

PRIVATE TRUCK

MILITARY ASSAULT FORCE

WILDLIFE CONSERVATIONIST

LIONS OF VIRGINIA

FRATERNAL PLATE

COLLEGIATE PLATE
"THE UNIVERSITY"

SERVICE ACADEMY

The "Old Dominion State" issues two fully-reflectorized license plates. Passenger plates are issued three alpha-three numeric, and all numeric plates. Virginia coined the term "communiplate" to promote personalized plate sales.

Distinctive captions:

DELEGATE - Member Virginia House of Delegates.
DRIVE AWAY -Transporter / repossessor.
HOBBYIST - Reconstructed car at least 20 years old.
MILITARY ASSAULT FORCE- Member of any unit involved in combat (Desert Storm, Panama, Grenada etc.)

SHERIFF - Sheriff, private vehicle.
POW - Former prisoner of war.
POSTMASTER- Local postal official .
REACT TEAM - Radio emergency group.
RIDE SHARING - Car pool
WILDLIFE CONSERVATIONIST - Active member of a conservation group such as Ducks Unlimited.

Codes:

Regular passenger car plates have 3 alpha - 3 numeric characters. Trucks and other commercial vehicle plates have a 1 or 2 alpha prefix followed by numerics.

The following alpha prefixes have special significance:

AF	Air Force Reserve	**M**	Municipal	**TA - TZ**	Truck
AR	Army Reserve	**MC**	Motorcycle	**TH**	Truck for hire
CG	Coast Guard "	**MR**	Marine Reserve	**TR**	Trailer
D	Dealer	**NG**	National Guard	**TRH**	Trailer for hire
DA	Drive away	**NR**	Naval Reserve	**UD**	Used car dealer
E	Regular bus	**P**	Apportioned truck	**UR**	Univ. of Richmond
EA	Apportioned bus	**POW**	Former pris of war	**W&L**	Wash. & Lee Univ.
EQ	Equipment	**PV**	Ride sharing	**W&M**	William & Mary
F	Farm truck	**PY**	Apportnd. trk., tlr.	**X**	Temporary tag
FD	Franchise dealer	**R**	Rental truck	**XA - XZ**	Tractor for hire
H	Taxi	**RT**	R.E.A.C.T team	**Y**	Tractor
HA - HZ	Truck for hire	**RA**	Rental trailer	**YH**	Tractor for hire
HI	Hearing impaired	**RAA-RZZ**	Rental passenger	**1A**	Lt. Governor
HO	Hobbyist	**RH**	Trailer for hire		
HP	Handicapped	**RS**	Rescue squad		
ID	Import dealer	**RX**	Pharmacist		

Passenger cars and trucks 7500lbs and under are issued plates from these series:

1-10,000 (all numeric)
A2 - A10,000 (A1 issued to Attorney General)
AAA 1-ZZZ 999
T1 -T500 (pickup or panel truck only)

Low numbers are reserved and issued as personalized plates.

Personalized plate request forms are available from Dept. of Motor Vehicles,P.O.Box 27412, Richmond 23269 of from any license agent or branch office. 2-7 characters available. Annual $10 fee plus regular registration cost. Collegiate plates $25, personalized collegiate $35 - both are annual fees.

To trace the owner of a Virginia registered vehicle write to Commonwealth of Virginia, Department of Motor Vehicles, P.O.Box 27412, Richmond. Give the plate number and request an abstract of the registration. Enclose a $5 fee for every record. You must explain your reason for the inquiry.

WASHINGTON

STATE ROUTE MARKER

3

★ KGA 1510 Spokane
KTAC 850 Tacoma
KIXI 880 Seattle
KING 1090 Seattle

AM RADIO

SEATTLE
TACOMA
SPOKANE

MO Washington YR
523-DYZZ

2 PLATES VALIDATED
BY 2 DECALS ON
REAR PLATE

WASHINGTON MO/YR
A BC 123

OLDER ISSUE
STILL IN USE

MO Washington YR
123-CBA
Centennial Celebration

PASSENGER PLATE
(CENTENNIAL CELEBRATION
DELETED DURING 1991)

MO Washington YR
MARTHA
Centennial Celebration

PERSONALIZED

MO Washington YR
1234 DP
Centennial Celebration

DISABLED PERSON

MO Washington YR
XMT 68098D
Centennial Celebration

TAX EXEMPT VEHICLE
SUFFIX E, K, M-STATE
C-COUNTY, D-CITY

MO Washington YR
XMT 432WSP
Centennial Celebration

STATE PATROL
LINE TROOPER

MO Washington YR
XMT 4326SP
Centennial Celebration

VEHICLE REGISTERED
TO STATE PATROL DEPT.

MO Washington YR
85632-L
Centennial Celebration

TRUCK

MO Washington YR
7890-JX
Centennial Celebration

TRAILER

19 Washington YR
12345PR
APPORTIONED

APPORTIONED
POWER UNIT

19 Washington YR
12345TR
APPORTIONED

APPORTIONED
TRAILER UNIT

MO Washington YR
HLK 0010A
Centennial Celebration

HULK HAULER

MO Washington YR
2165-PW
Centennial Celebration

PRISONER OF WAR

MO Washington YR
PEARL HARBOR SURVIVOR 123
Centennial Celebration

PEARL HARBOR SURVIVOR

WASHINGTON PERMANENT REGISTRATION
MEDAL OF HONOR ★★★★★ 1

CONGRESSIONAL
MEDAL OF HONOR
RECIPIENT

The "Evergreen State" issues two fully-reflectorized license plates. Washington has not had a general plate re-issue since 1963 and there are five different bases currently in use. Personalized plates come in a choice of colors.

Distinctive captions:

DLR - Dealer
HORSELESS CARRIAGE - Vehicle manufactured 1931 or earlier.
HLK - Hulk hauler
MISC - Miscellaneous dealer.
TRAN - Transporter
XMT - Tax exempt - Government vehicle
    (including Indian tribal government)
    (prefix or suffix)   **D** - city vehicle
                      C - County vehicle
              E, K, M - State vehicle
WKR - Wrecker / dismantler

Codes:

Passenger vehicle plates have 3 alpha- 3 numeric and 3 numeric - 3 alpha characters. On older plates the first 2 alpha characters was a county code. Some of these plates are still in use but the codes are no longer accurate. The current issue of graphic (mountain background) plates have no county codes and the most recent version the words *Centennial Celebration* no longer appear at the bottom.

There are special low number plates available for the following State officials:

1. Governor
2. Lt. Governor
3. Secretary of State

4. State Treasurer
5. State Auditor
6. Attorney General

7. Supt. Pub. Instruction
8. Land Commissioner
9. Insurance Comm.

Trucks, trailers, buses, publicly owned and special vehicle plates have 1 or 2 alpha prefix or (suffix) which indicate as follows:

A	Truck	**G, GA - GZ**	Truck	**Q**	Trailer
B	State owned	**HA - HZ**	Diesel truck	**SP**	State Patrol Dept
C	County	**I**	Indian exempt	**T, U**	Truck
CC	Hon. Consul	**J, JA - JZ**	Trailer	**V**	Travel trailer
D	City owned	**K**	State owned	**WSP**	State Trooper
DV	Disabled vetrn.	**L, LA - LZ**	Truck	**W, WA - WZ**	Travel Trailer
DP	Disabled per.	**M**	State owned	**X, XA - XZ**	Truck
F, FA -FZ	Trailer	**P, PA - PZ**	Truck	**Z**	Trailer

Personalized plates are available from Personalized Plate Desk, Dept. of Licensing, Olympia 98504. One can select 1 - 7 green alpha and/or numeric characters on either a yellow background or blue characters on Centennial. The fee is $30 plus regular registration. Profit goes to wildlife species program.

To trace the owner write to: Dept. of Licensing Records Section, P.O.Box 9909 Olympia 98507-9038. The fee is $2 per record request and $1.50 per printout.

WEST VIRGINIA

STATE ROUTE MARKER

32

WHEELING

PARKERSBURG

CHARLESTON

★ **WWVA 1170** Wheeling
WCHS 580 Charleston
WADC 1050 Parkersburg

AM RADIO

1 PLATE VALIDATED
BY 1 DECAL

PASSENGER OLDER
ISSUE STILL IN USE

PERSONALIZED

HANDICAPPED PERSON

FRONT PLATE ON
STATE CAR

DISABLED VETERAN

NATIONAL GUARD

COUNTY OWNED, ALPHA
PREFIXES INDICATE CLASS

TRUCK NOT FOR HIRE

UNIVERSITY
OWNED VEHICLE

EMERGENCY MEDICAL
SERVICE

POLICE ASSOCIATION

COLLEGIATE

PEARL HARBOR SURVIVOR

PURPLE HEART RECIPIENT

VETERAN

106

The "Mountain State" issues one fully-reflectorized license plate. West Virginia has not had a general re-issue since 1976, and there are three base plate designs in use.

Distinctive captions:

ANTIQUE CAR: Vehicle at least 25 years old.
NON-RESIDENT - Non-residents with temporary and recurring business in the state of West Virginia.
REPOSSESSOR - Vehicle repossessed by bank or lending institution.

Codes:

All West Virginia class "A" plates (Passenger type motor vehicles and pickup trucks up to 8,000 lbs GVW other than those for hire) receive 1 numeric and 1 alpha, or 2 alpha prefix followed by 4 numerics. The first character in the prefix indicates the month expiration. Plates expire on the first day of the month.

1 - January	**4** - April	**7** - July	**O** - October
2 - February	**5** - May	**8** - August	**N** - November
3 - March	**6** - June	**9** - September	**D** - December

The year expiration decal changes every calendar year.

A second type of "A" plate is all numeric. Plate numbers 2 - 2,000 (without prefix) are assigned to individuals by the Governor. The Governor receives plate 1 and ONE.

Trucks, truck tractors and road tractors (other than those leased for hire) are issued plates with a B prefix followed by 1 - 5 numerics.
The numerics are for individual vehicle identification only. When registrations in this class exceed 5 figures, a small numeric indicating 100,000 is embossed under the B prefix.

All other vehicles are issued plates using a similar numbering system with an alpha prefix which indicates as follows:

C - Trailers, semi-trailers not for hire.
D - Dealers (other alphas show type)
DV - Reserved for disabled veterans
E - Trucks , tractors exempt from Public Service Comm. jurisdiction.
H - Taxis and buses.
J - Charter buses and cars.
K - Leased or for hire trucks, tractors.

L - Trailers, semi-trailers for hire.
R - House trailers
S - Special mobile equipment
T - Light trailers and semi-trailers (under 1 Ton) drawn by pass. cars.
POW - Ex prisoner of war.
X - Farm truck

West Virginia does not designate the county of origin or weight of a vehicle on the license plate.

Personalized plates available from Special License Clerk, Div. of Motor Vehicles Capital Complex Bldg 3, Charleston 25317. 2 - 6 characters are permitted the fee is an additional $15 per year.

To trace the owner of a West Virginia plate, citizens are requested to contact law enforcement agencies. In special cases contact DMV in Charleston with an explanation.

WISCONSIN

STATE ROUTE MARKER

22

WCUB 980 Manitowoc
WISN 1130 Milwaukee
WGEE 1360 Green Bay
WIZM 1410 La Crosse

GREEN BAY
LA CROSSE
MANITOWOC
MILWAUKEE

AM RADIO

WISCONSIN
HBC-123
JAN · America's Dairyland · 91

2 PLATES VALIDATED BY
2 DECALS ON REAR PLATE

AMERICA'S DAIRYLAND
A10-001
JAN · WISCONSIN · 91

PASSENGER REGULAR
1979 ISSUE ALSO
2 ALPHA - 4 NUMERIC

WISCONSIN
ABC-123
JAN · America's Dairyland · 91

PASSENGER REGULAR
1986 ISSUE
3 ALPHA - 3 NUMERIC

WISCONSIN
DAIRY
JAN · America's Dairyland · 91

PERSONALIZED

WISCONSIN
D¹S1001
JAN · America's Dairyland · 91

DISABLED

· DISABLED VETERAN ·
VET 12
JAN · WISCONSIN · 91

DISABLED VETERAN

OFFICIAL
★ 1
JAN · WISCONSIN · 91

STATE PATROL

EX-PRISONER OF WAR
POW-1
AUG · WISCONSIN · YR

EX-PRISONER OF WAR

STATE OWNED
1001
WISCONSIN

STATE OWNED VEHICLE

TRACTOR
TA 1
WISCONSIN · 91

SEMI-TRACTOR POWER

WIS
A123
MENOMINEE NATION

TRIBAL PLATE

· APPORTIONED ·
100001
TRL · WISCONSIN · 91

INTERSTATE TRAILER

· FINANCE CO ·
5001 A
JAN · WISCONSIN · 91

REPOSSESSOR

· MEDAL OF HONOR ·
2
WISCONSIN

CONGRESSIONAL
MEDAL OF HONOR
RECIPIENT

KOREAN WAR VETERAN
20001
AUG · WISCONSIN · YR

KOREAN WAR VETERAN

UNIVERSITY
RF123
JAN · WISCONSIN · 91

COLLEGIATE PLATE
STANDARD BASE
(RIVER FALLS UNIVERSITY)

108

"America's Dairyland" issues two fully-reflectorized license plates. Wisconsin has not had a general plate re-issue since 1980 and there are three different passenger base plate designs in use. All the black on yellow passenger plates to be replaced by 1993.

Distinctive captions:

ANTIQUE : 40 year old vehicle
COLLECTOR : 20 year old vehicle
DUAL PURPOSE VEH: Truck
also used as a motor home.
DUAL PURPOSE FARM: Truck
for farm and other uses.
FINANCE CO - Repossessor.
GUARD MEMBER: Wisconsin National
Guard member.

HOBBYIST : Vehicle 20 yrs old
reconstructed or homemade.
OFFICIAL : State or municipal vehicle
used in law enforcement.
TRANSF TRLR: Used to transport
modular housing units.

Codes:

Wisconsin passenger plates now have a decal that shows the expiration month. On earlier issues of Wisconsin plates (1979 black on yellow base) the expiration month was shown in an alpha prefix code.

Trucks and other commercial vehicle plates are clearly captioned to show class of vehicle such as truck, trailer tractor etc. However on heavy vehicles the top alpha prefix is a code for the registered gross weight:

Z - 3,000 Lbs.	**F** - 20,000	**N** - 56,000
A - 4,500	**G** - 26,000	**P** - 62,000
B - 6,000	**H** - 22,000	**Q** - 68,000
C - 8,000	**J** - 38,000	**R** - 73,000
D - 12,000	**K** - 44,000	**S** - 76,000
E - 16,000	**L** - 50,000	**T** - 80,000

Wisconsin reserves the following prefix combinations for use on special plates:

BX - Bus (urban mass transit system)
DIS - Disabled person
EMT - Emergency medical technician
M over **H** - Mobile home
VET - Disabled veteran

X (suffix) - Vehicles registered at
reduced fee.
ZY - Vehicle used to transport elderly
and/or disabled persons.

Personalized plate request forms are available from Registration Services,Wisc. Dept. of Transportation, P.O.Box 9711, Madison 53707. 2 - 6 alpha/numeric characters can be requested. Extra fee $10 annually. Wisconsin offers collegiate plates at an additional charge.

To trace the owner of a Wisconsin plate write to: Vehicle Files< Wisc. Dept. of Transportation, P.O.Box 7911, Madison 53707. Fee $2.00 per record, plus 5% tax for Wisconsin residents only.

WYOMING

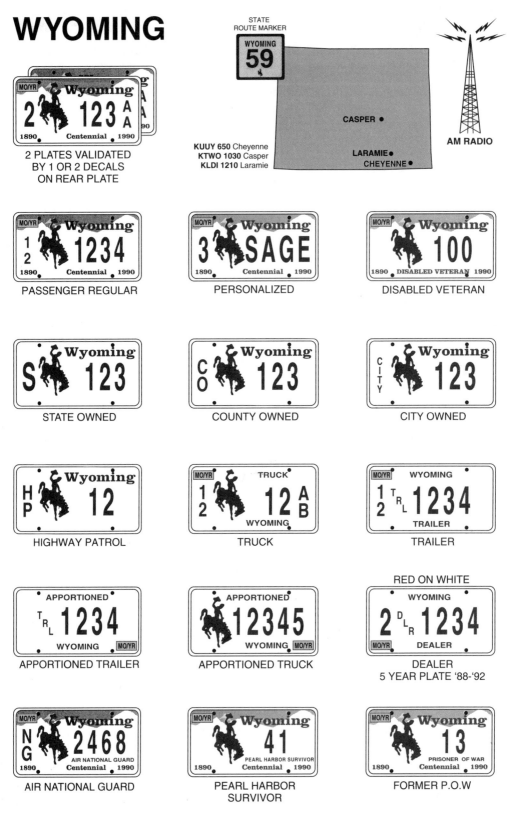

STATE ROUTE MARKER

WYOMING 59

KUUY 650 Cheyenne
KTWO 1030 Casper
KLDI 1210 Laramie

CASPER
LARAMIE
CHEYENNE

AM RADIO

2 PLATES VALIDATED
BY 1 OR 2 DECALS
ON REAR PLATE

PASSENGER REGULAR

PERSONALIZED

DISABLED VETERAN

STATE OWNED

COUNTY OWNED

CITY OWNED

HIGHWAY PATROL

TRUCK

TRAILER

APPORTIONED TRAILER

APPORTIONED TRUCK

DEALER
5 YEAR PLATE '88-'92

RED ON WHITE

AIR NATIONAL GUARD

PEARL HARBOR
SURVIVOR

FORMER P.O.W

WYOMING

The "Equality State" issues two fully-reflectorized license plates. Wyoming has featured the bucking bronco on its plates since 1936. A county code number appears to the left of the bronco. A new general issue of graphic plates is scheduled for 1993.

Distinctive captions:
PIONEER: Vehicle at least 25 years old.
COML: Commercial vehicle
SCHOOL: School district vehicle

Codes:
All Wyoming private and commercial license plates are issued by county treasurers and they have a numeric prefix which identifies the issuing county. Wyoming has 23 counties and the code, county and (county seat) are listed below:

Prefix	County	County seat
1	Natrona	Casper
2	Laramie	Cheyenne
3	Sheridan	Sheridan
4	Sweetwater	Rock Springs
5	Albany	Laramie
6	Carbon	Rawlins
7	Goshen	Torrington
8	Platte	Wheatland
9	Big Horn	Basin
10	Fremont	Lander
11	Park	Cody
12	Lincoln	Kemmerer
13	Converse	Douglas
14	Niobrara	Lusk
15	Hot Springs	Thermopolis
16	Johnson	Buffalo
17	Campbell	Gillette
18	Crook	Sundance
19	Uinta	Evanston
20	Washakie	Worland
21	Weston	Newcastle
22	Teton	Jackson
23	Sublette	Pinedale
99	Rental fleet vehicle	

Amateur radio, apportioned and pioneer plates have no county code.
Air National Guard plates have all even numerics; Army Guard has all odd.

State and other government owned vehicle plates have prefix codes. Multiple character prefixes are stacked:

CC - Community college
CO - County owned
EX - Vehicle exempt from registr. fee
FD - Fire Dept
GCD - Civil Defense
GF - Game and fish
GFD - Govt. Forestry Div.
H - Highway Dept.
HD - Highway Dept. headquarters vehicle
HP - Highway Patrol
S - State owned vehicle
UW - University of Wyoming
WP - Weed and Pest Control

Alpha codes are used instead of the bucking bronco symbol on plates issued to these classes of vehicles:

GFD - Government Forestry Div. , **MFG** - Manufacturer ,
TRL - Trailer, DLR -Dealer, **HT** - House trailer

Personalized plates are available from Wyoming Dept of Transportation, MV Licensing and Titling Section, 5300 Bishop Blvd., Cheyenne WY. 82002- 9019. 1-4 alpha/numeric characters plus county prefix are allowed. No more than 2 "M's" or "W's" can be used. The additional fee is $30 every 5 years.

To trace a Wyoming plate contact the MV Licensing & Titling Section in Cheyenne (see address above and request the information. There is a $5 search charge per record.

ALBERTA

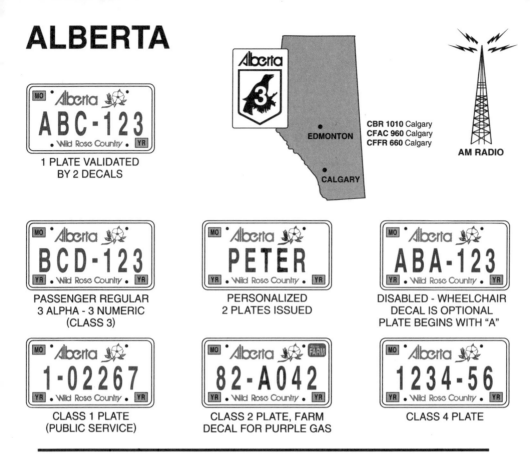

1 PLATE VALIDATED
BY 2 DECALS

CBR 1010 Calgary
CFAC 960 Calgary
CFFR 660 Calgary

AM RADIO

PASSENGER REGULAR
3 ALPHA - 3 NUMERIC
(CLASS 3)

PERSONALIZED
2 PLATES ISSUED

DISABLED - WHEELCHAIR
DECAL IS OPTIONAL
PLATE BEGINS WITH "A"

CLASS 1 PLATE
(PUBLIC SERVICE)

CLASS 2 PLATE, FARM
DECAL FOR PURPLE GAS

CLASS 4 PLATE

Alberta issues the same Wild Rose Country graphic design plate to all classes of vehicles. Whenever captions are used they appear on the upper right corner and are self-explanatory. Passenger car plates are 3 alpha - 3 numeric, and no codes are used.

Alberta has four regular classes and six special plates. The regular classes can be identified by a spacer dot •.

Class 1 (Public Service vehicles) One numeric followed by a dot i.e. **1• 12345**
Buses, livery, car rental, truck rental, public service trailer, driveaway etc.

Class 2 2 numerics followed by dot i.e. **12•1234.**
Farm vehicle, nurseryman, transport own goods,priv. bus, gen. merch. for hire.

Class 3 3 alpha dot 3 numerics i.e. **ABC•123.**
Passenger, motorcycle, Govt, driveaway, transport own goods, comm. trailer

Class 4 4 numerics dot 2 numerics i.e. **1234 • 56**
Trailers

Special plates are: Antique, Consular ,Dealer, Disabled Ham radio. All are captioned.

License plates are issued at random within a class, therefore it is not possible to distinguish between types. For example a rental car , a livery and a driveaway are all class 1 and have a single numeric prefix. No other codes are used. Prefix VE6 reserved for ham radio operators.

Personalized plates are available from any Motor Vehicle License Issue Office. Any combination of up to 7 alpha numeric characters can be requested. The initial fee is $165 plus tax.

To trace the owner of an Alberta registered vehicle contact the Search Unit MVD North Office, 10125 Princess Elizabeth Ave. Edmonton T5G OX9 (403) 422-2250, or Search Unit MVD Calgary , 4020 Bowness Rd. Calgary T3B OA2 94 tel (403) 297-4210.

BRITISH COLUMBIA

2 PLATES VALIDATED BY 1 DECAL REAR PLATE

Beautiful British Columbia
ABC ≋ 123
MO/YR

99 B.C.

CBU 690 Vancouver
CKDA 1220 Victoria

VANCOUVER
VICTORIA

AM RADIO

HEATHER
BRITISH   COLUMBIA
PERSONALIZED

Beautiful British Columbia
VE70V
MO/YR
AMATEUR RADIO

Beautiful British Columbia
CONSUL 382
MO/YR
FOREIGN CONSUL

Beautiful British Columbia
7924 ≋ NN
MO/YR
COMMERCIAL TRUCK

Beautiful British Columbia
A7 ≋ 5634
MO/YR
FARM TRUCK

VINTAGE
4158
BRITISH COLUMBIA
ANTIQUE CAR

British Columbia issues 3 alpha - 3 numeric plates to passenger vehicles. There are no county of origin, weight or special use codes. The plate characters are for individual vehicle identification only.

Trucks, trailers and other commercial vehicle tags are 2 alpha - 4 numeric and these codes are used:

Prefix	**Suffix**
A - Farm truck	2 ALPHA - Commercial truck
D - Demonstrator	1 Numeric 1 Alpha - Commercial trailer
F - Farm tractor	**SA** - Special agreement plate- for mining
MA - Auto. manufacturer	equipment limited use of the highway.
R - Repairman	
P - Prorated	
TF - Trailer floater	
TR - Transporter	
X - Industrial equipment.	

The weight of a vehicle does not appear on a B.C.license plate.

Personalized plates (PNP) are available from The Insurance Corporation of B.C., Room 135-151 West Esplanade, N. Vancouver B.C. V7M-3H9. 2 - 6 alpha numeric characters can be requested. The initial fee is $50, and $24 annual renewal.

To Trace the owner of a vehicle through the plate number, one should contact Vehicle Services Dept, Motor Vehicles Branch in Victoria. Information not available to the general public, only authorized persons, and for a valid reason. A fee is charged for this service.

MANITOBA

YELLOWHEAD ROUTE
YELLOWHEAD
16
MANITOBA

CBW 990 Winnipeg
CJOB 680 Winnipeg
CKY 580 Winnipeg

WINNIPEG

AM RADIO

123 ABC — FRIENDLY — YR MANITOBA YR
1 PLATE VALIDATED BY YEAR DECAL

123 ABC — FRIENDLY — YR MANITOBA YR
PASSENGER - 1983 ISSUE 2 PLATES

123 ABC — FRIENDLY — MANITOBA
PASSENGER - 1987 ISSUE 2 PLATES - 1-3 NUMERIC

BISON — FRIENDLY — YR MANITOBA
PERSONALIZED CAN BE ON 1983 OR 1987 BASE

123 ABC FRIENDLY YR MANITOBA
HANDICAPPED PERSON REGULAR PLATE SPECIAL STICKER

123 TAA — FRIENDLY — YR MANITOBA
LOCAL TRUCK SUFFIX BEGINS WITH LETTER "T"

123 CWA CT YR MANITOBA
COMMERCIAL TRUCK

Manitoba passenger plates have 1 - 3 numeric followed by 3 alpha characters. There are no county codes on passenger plates. Commercial and public service vehicles are identified by captions. Codes are used on other plates:

Captions:		**Codes: (suffix)**	
CT	Commercial truck	AEA-AEX	Veh. owned by Manitoba
CT-TL	Commercial trailer	MD	Medical doctor
CT-D	Commercial driveaway	VE4	Amateur radio operator
CT-DX	Comm. driveaway out-of-prov.	C over T	Comm. Truck quarterly registration
LIV	Livery	D	Dealer
PSV	"For Hire" vehicle	F	Farm vehicle
PSV-D	"For Hire" driveaway	P over S	Public serv. truck qtr. registration
PSV-TL	"For Hire" trailer	P over X	Pub. Sv. Trk. out-of prov. use.
PSV-X	"For Hire" veh. out-of-prov use.	T	Local Truck
		U	Rental vehicle
		R	Repairman

Apportioned plates display a special "CAVR" sticker top left on the plate.
Handicapped persons have a special sticker for the top left of their plate.

Personalized plate applications available at AUTOPAC insurance, or Dept of Highways and Transportation, Div. of Driver and Vehicle Licensing 1075 Portage Ave. Winnipeg R3G OS1. One time fee of $75. 6 characters allowed.

To trace the owner one must visit Motor Vehicle Div, Portage Ave Winnipeg, present identification, give the reason and pay a $4 fee.

NEW BRUNSWICK

AAA-123

2 PLATES VALIDATED
BY 1 DECAL ON
BOTH PLATES

CBA **1070** Moncton
CFNB **550** Fredericton
CFBC **930** Saint John

MONCTON
FREDERICTON
SAINT JOHN

TRANS CANADA 2

AM RADIO

New Nouveau **Brunswick** — MO/YR

FUNDY
PERSONALIZED

AMPUTEE
AM1-151
AMPUTEE

ANTIQUE
AA1-234
ANTIQUE AUTO

1
LIEUTENANT GOVERNOR

CAA-123
LT. COMMERCIAL VEHICLE

VE1PJJ
CALL-SIGN
INDICATIF D'APPEL

TAA-001
TRAILER

L50-001
LARGE COMMERCIAL VEHICLE

DP-301
DIPLOMAT

New Brunswick issues 3 alpha - 3 numeric character plates to passenger vehicles, beginning at BAA-001. These plates were first issued on May 1 1991 and will replace all previous 1986 series (blue & green on white) plate by April 30, 1992. They do not contain any county, weight or use codes. Light commercial, prorated truck, and trailers now have a 3 alpha prefix while other types have a 1 or 2 alpha prefix. The special prefixes used on New Brunswick license plates are:

AA - Antique Auto
AM - Amputee
D - Dealer
DP - Diplomat
CAA* - Lt. comm. vehicle
F - Farm truck
H - Taxi

HA - Transportor
L - Large commercial vehicle
M - Special mobile equipment
P - Farm produce transporter
PRA*- Prorated vehicle
TA - Trailer
TAA* - Trailer

Personalized plates are available from Motor Vehicle Branch P.O.Box 6000 Fredericton E3B 5H1. 7 characters permitted, cost $139.10 for the life of the plate (5 - 8 years). Vehicle registration fees are additional.
To trace the owner of a plate contact MVB in Fredericton. Give the reason for the inquiry. The search fee is $7.

NEWFOUNDLAND
AND LABRADOR

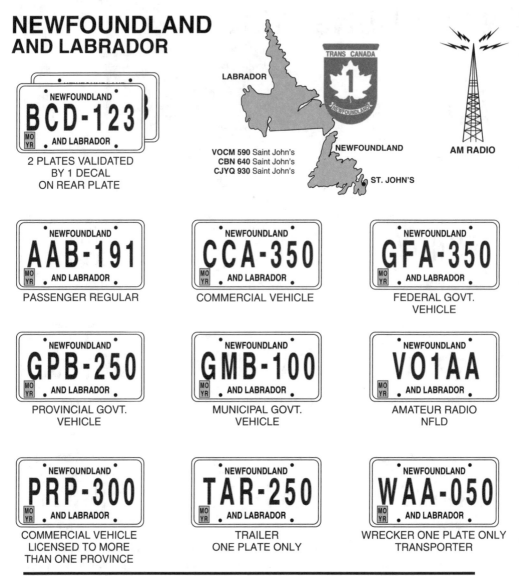

NEWFOUNDLAND
BCD-123
AND LABRADOR
2 PLATES VALIDATED
BY 1 DECAL
ON REAR PLATE

TRANS CANADA
1

LABRADOR

VOCM 590 Saint John's
CBN 640 Saint John's
CJYQ 930 Saint John's

NEWFOUNDLAND

ST. JOHN'S

AM RADIO

NEWFOUNDLAND
AAB-191
AND LABRADOR
PASSENGER REGULAR

NEWFOUNDLAND
CCA-350
AND LABRADOR
COMMERCIAL VEHICLE

NEWFOUNDLAND
GFA-350
AND LABRADOR
FEDERAL GOVT.
VEHICLE

NEWFOUNDLAND
GPB-250
AND LABRADOR
PROVINCIAL GOVT.
VEHICLE

NEWFOUNDLAND
GMB-100
AND LABRADOR
MUNICIPAL GOVT.
VEHICLE

NEWFOUNDLAND
VO1AA
AND LABRADOR
AMATEUR RADIO
NFLD

NEWFOUNDLAND
PRP-300
AND LABRADOR
COMMERCIAL VEHICLE
LICENSED TO MORE
THAN ONE PROVINCE

NEWFOUNDLAND
TAR-250
AND LABRADOR
TRAILER
ONE PLATE ONLY

NEWFOUNDLAND
WAA-050
AND LABRADOR
WRECKER ONE PLATE ONLY
TRANSPORTER

Newfoundland has one plate design that is issued to all vehicles. Plates have 3 alpha- 3 numeric characters. There are no codes used for county of origin, weight or use restrictions. Alpha prefixes with special meaning:

C - Commercial vehicle
DAA - Dealer
F, FAA-FZZ - Farm, forestry, mining vehicle
GF - Federal government vehicle
GP - Provincial government vehicle
GM - Municipal government vehicle
MHA - Member of House Assembly

PRP - Prorated vehicle
T - Trailer
VO1 - Ham radio (Newfoundland)
VO2 - Ham radio (Labrador)
W - Wrecker
X - Construction equipment
D - Dealer demonstrator plate

Newfoundland does not issue personalized license plates. Quebec is the only other jurisdiction in North America who also does not offer these tags.

To trace the owner of a Newfoundland vehicle one must contact Govt. of Newfoundland Motor Registration Division. Box 8710 , St. John's Nfld. A1B 4J5. A legal reason must be given, so it is best to inquire through a law enforcement agency. Fee is $5.

NOVA SCOTIA

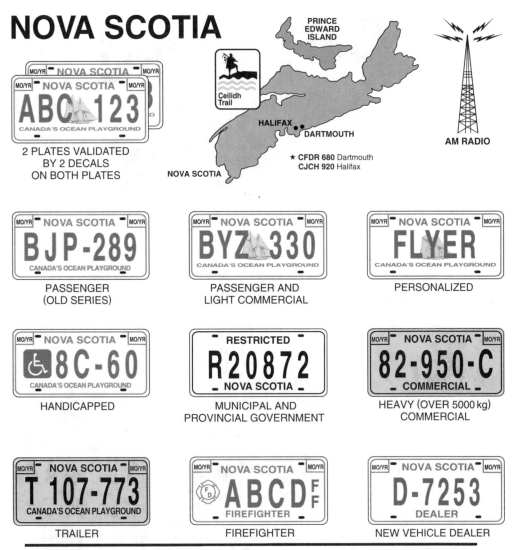

2 PLATES VALIDATED
BY 2 DECALS
ON BOTH PLATES

**PASSENGER
(OLD SERIES)**

**PASSENGER AND
LIGHT COMMERCIAL**

PERSONALIZED

HANDICAPPED

**MUNICIPAL AND
PROVINCIAL GOVERNMENT**

**HEAVY (OVER 5000 kg)
COMMERCIAL**

TRAILER

FIREFIGHTER

NEW VEHICLE DEALER

All Nova Scotia plates are used for many years and revalidated by decals. Passenger plates have 3 alpha - 3 numeric characters and have no codes. The graphic (Schooner "Bluenose") is the most recent issue, however older passenger plates are still on the road. Heavy trucks,trailers and other commercial vehicles over 5000 Kg. plates are a different color - black on yellow. Government vehicle plates are black on white, and prorated plates red on yellow. The alpha prefixes reserved for special use:

D -New car dealer (blue on white)
F/F - (suffix) Firefighter
FM - Farm truck (blue on white)
FT - Farm tractor (black on yellow)
GT - General tractor (blue on white)

PRP - Prorated (red on yellow)
PT - Semi-trailer (black on yellow) undated
R - Government (black on white)
T - Trailer (black on yellow)
U - Used car dealer
VE1 - Ham radio

Personalized plates are available through Registry of Motor Vehicles, Licenses and Registrations, Halifax B3J 2Z3. 2 - 7 characters permitted. Fee $70 for purchase of special plate, plus annual $20 use fee. Tax and vehicle registration fees additional

To trace the owner of a plate, the public is not permitted free access to this information. Requests are best made through a law enforcement agency.

ONTARIO

CFRB 1010 Toronto
CFTR 680 Toronto
CFGO 1200 Ottawa
CKLW 800 Windsor

OTTOWA

WINDSOR   TORONTO

AM RADIO

123 ◆ ABC
YOURS TO DISCOVER

2 PLATES VALIDATED BY 1 DECAL
ON REAR PLATE OF PASSENGER
AND FRONT PLATE OF
COMMERCIAL VEHICLES

123 ◆ ABC
YOURS TO DISCOVER

PASSENGER REGULAR
3 ALPHA - 3 NUMERIC

ABC ◆ 123
KEEP IT BEAUTIFUL

PASSENGER REGULAR
OLDER ISSUE PLATE

KEITH
YOURS TO DISCOVER

PERSONALIZED

001 ◆ CDA
YOURS TO DISCOVER

DIPLOMATIC CORPS.

ONA ◆ 001
YOURS TO DISCOVER

ONTARIO GOVERNMENT

MHC ◆ 001
YOURS TO DISCOVER

MEMBERS OF HOUSE
OF COMMONS

SEN ◆ 001
YOURS TO DISCOVER

SENATOR

DLA ◆ 123
YOURS TO DISCOVER

DEALER

VE3 ◆ AAA
AMATEUR RADIO

AMATEUR RADIO

Ontario license plates have 6 characters divided by a crown. Passenger are 3 numeric - 3 alpha and there are no codes. Earlier issue 3 alpha 3 numeric plates are still in use. Passenger plates are blue on white, commercial are black on white and diplomatic white on red. The following alpha code appear as either a prefix or suffix

CAN -Fed. govt cabinet
CCA (suffix only)- Consular Corps (white on red)
CDA (suffix only)- Diplomatic Corp (white on red)
XTR (suffix only)- Foreign nationals (white on red)
DCO (suffix only) - District Court Judge
DLA - DLZ (prefix or suffix) Dealer
FCJ - Fed. Court Judge
FDA - Federal Govt vehicle
HVA - Historic vehicle

MDA,MAA - Medical doctor
MHC - Member House Commons
MPP - Ontario legislature
ONA - Ontario govt. veh
ONT - Ontario govt cabinet
PJO - Ontario provincial Judge
SCO - Ont. Supreme Court Judge
SEN - Senate members
TRB - Tax Review Board
VE3 - Amateur Radio

Personalized plates are available from Ministry of Transportation 2680 Keele St. Downsview Ont. M3M 3E6. The cost is $100 for the life of the plate. Vehicle registration fees are extra. Up to 6 alpha/numeric characters allowed.

To trace an Ontario plate contact Vehicles Search Div, at Keele St. address. Information on available for a legitimate legal reason. Fee is $5.

PRINCE EDWARD ISLAND

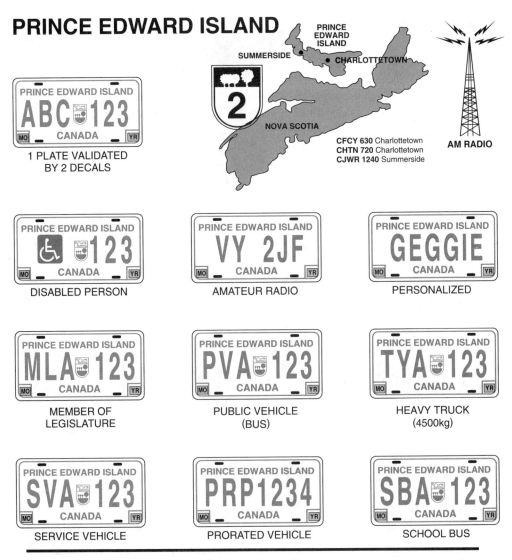

1 PLATE VALIDATED BY 2 DECALS

CFCY 630 Charlottetown
CHTN 720 Charlottetown
CJWR 1240 Summerside

AM RADIO

DISABLED PERSON

AMATEUR RADIO

PERSONALIZED

MEMBER OF LEGISLATURE

PUBLIC VEHICLE (BUS)

HEAVY TRUCK (4500kg)

SERVICE VEHICLE

PRORATED VEHICLE

SCHOOL BUS

Prince Edward Island has only one plate design which includes a coat-of arms in the center. Passenger plates are 3 alpha- 3 numeric and have no codes. These are alpha prefixes that are reserved for special use:

DLR - Dealers
FAA - Farm vehicle
FTA - Fire truck
GSA - Government service
MC - Motorcycle
MLA - Legislator

PEI - Provincial Cabinet
PRP - Prorated
PVA - Public vehicle
SBA - School bus
SMA - Special mobile equip.
SVA - Service vehicle

TRA-TRZ - Trailer
TY - 1/3 year heavy truck
VY2 - Ham radio call letters

Personalized plates are available through Highway Safety Div. Box 2000 Charlottetown C1A 7N8. 7 alpha numeric characters allowed. The cost is $100 for the plate and $20 annual use fee, plus normal vehicle registration fees.

To trace the owner of a vehicle through the plate number, it is best to contact law enforcement agencies. P.E.I does not offer this service to the general public. When an authorized agency inquires, they are charged a $10 search fee.

QUEBEC

112

★ **CBF 690** Montreal
★ **CBM 940** Montreal
CJAD 800 Montreal
CIBM 1310 Riviere du Loup

RIVIERE DE LOUP

MONTREAL

AM RADIO

Quebec
ABC 123
Je me souviens — MO

1 PLATE VALIDATED
BY 1 DECAL

Quebec YR
ABC 123
Je me souviens

HANDICAPPED PERSON
WHEELCHAIR STICKER
UPPER RT. HAND CORNER

79 **Quebec**
F-AB1234
Je me souviens — MO

COMMERCIAL VEHICLE

79 **Quebec**
C-123456
Je me souviens — MO

RESTRICTED TRAVEL PLATE
(COLLECTOR VEHICLE)

79 **Quebec**
L-A123456
Je me souviens — MO

TRUCK

Quebec
L-A123456
Je me souviens — MO

TRUCK
PERMANENT PLATE

79 **Quebec** PRP
L-123456
Je me souviens — MO

TRUCK PRORATED

79 **Quebec**
T36-1234
Je me souviens — MO

URBAN TAXI

79 **Quebec**
A-12345
Je me souviens — MO

SCHOOL BUS

79 **Quebec**
CC-123
Je me souviens — MO

CONSULAR OFFICIAL

Quebec license plates all have the same design. Passenger plates are 3 alpha - 3 numeric and do not contain any codes. The other categories of plates have an alpha prefix to identify the class followed by numerics that identifies the individual vehicle:

A - Buses: Public, private, school
C - Vehicles with restricted right of travel.
CC - Consular corps
CD - Diplomatic Corps
F - Leased vehicle
R - Trailers
T - Urban taxi

TR - Rural taxi
TS - Limousine
L - General merchandise transport
V - All terrain & antique auto
VR - Bulk transport
VY2 - Ham radio
X - Floater license plate.

Personalized plates. Quebec is one of only two jurisdictions in North America that does not issue personalized license plates.

To trace the owner of a Quebec registered vehicle, contact Societe de L'assurance Automobile du Quebec, 333 Boulevard Jean Lesage C.P. 19600, G1K-8J6.

SASKATCHEWAN

2 PLATES VALIDATED BY CLASS OF VEHICLE DECAL ON LOWER LEFT AND YEAR DECAL LOWER RIGHT

CBK 540 Regina
CKBI 900 Prince Albert
CFSL 1190 Weyburn

PRINCE ALBERT

REGINA

WEYBURN

AM RADIO

LT. GOVERNOR

MEDICAL DOCTOR

PERSONALIZED

DISABLED

COMMERCIAL TRUCK

FARM TRUCK

GOVERNMENT

COMMERCIAL TRAILER

LEASED VEHICLE

Saskatchewan license plates have 6 characters, 3 alpha- 3 numeric with a graphic wheat design separating the two groupings. The only exception is personalized and disabled person plates which have different character configurations and the wheat does not appear. License plates are issued as the applications are processed, there is no significance to the alpha numeric combinations. Different color alpha coded decals are used to indicate the class of vehicle:

Green on White stickers
PV - Private vehicle
T - Private trailer
GC - Government veh.
Blue on White Stickers
A - Commercial
AG - Public serv.veh

restricted use.
C - Commercial /restricted
D - Commercial/provincial
TS - Commercial trailer
L - Leased
LT - Leased trailer
PB - Public bus

PC - City bus
PS - School bus
PT - Public taxi
TS - Commercial trailer
Red on White
F - Farm
VE5 - Ham radio

Personalized plates are available form any Motor Vehicle branch office. Up to 6 characters are allowed and the one time fee is $80.25 including tax.

To trace the owner of a vehicle through the plate number it is best to work through a law enforcement agency. Registration information is not available to the general public.

NORTHWEST TERRITORIES

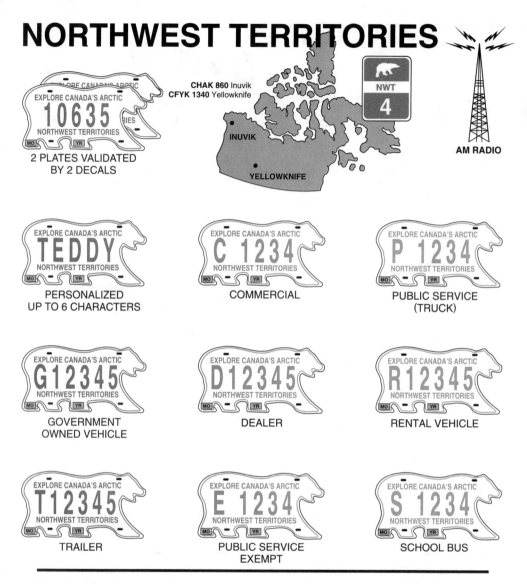

CHAK 860 Inuvik
CFYK 1340 Yellowknife

INUVIK

YELLOWKNIFE

NWT
4

AM RADIO

10635
NORTHWEST TERRITORIES
MO — YR

2 PLATES VALIDATED
BY 2 DECALS

EXPLORE CANADA'S ARCTIC
TEDDY
NORTHWEST TERRITORIES
MO — YR

PERSONALIZED
UP TO 6 CHARACTERS

EXPLORE CANADA'S ARCTIC
C 1234
NORTHWEST TERRITORIES
MO — YR

COMMERCIAL

EXPLORE CANADA'S ARCTIC
P 1234
NORTHWEST TERRITORIES
MO — YR

PUBLIC SERVICE
(TRUCK)

EXPLORE CANADA'S ARCTIC
G 12345
NORTHWEST TERRITORIES
MO — YR

GOVERNMENT
OWNED VEHICLE

EXPLORE CANADA'S ARCTIC
D 12345
NORTHWEST TERRITORIES
MO — YR

DEALER

EXPLORE CANADA'S ARCTIC
R 12345
NORTHWEST TERRITORIES
MO — YR

RENTAL VEHICLE

EXPLORE CANADA'S ARCTIC
T 12345
NORTHWEST TERRITORIES
MO — YR

TRAILER

EXPLORE CANADA'S ARCTIC
E 1234
NORTHWEST TERRITORIES
MO — YR

PUBLIC SERVICE
EXEMPT

EXPLORE CANADA'S ARCTIC
S 1234
NORTHWEST TERRITORIES
MO — YR

SCHOOL BUS

All Northwest Territories plates are in the shape of a polar bear. Regular passenger vehicle plates are all numeric and the numbers have no other significance other than to identify the individual vehicle. Commercial, government and other vehicle plates have a 1 alpha prefix code:

N.W.T does not issue special plates to disabled persons.

C - Commercial Vehicle
D - Dealer
E - Public service vehicle (exempt)
G - Government owned vehicle

P - Public service vehicle (truck)
R - Rental vehicle (Hertz etc.)
S - School bus
T -Trailer   **VE8** - Ham radio

Personalized plates are available from the Motor Vehicle Dept. in Yellowknife. Up to 6 alpha and /or numeric characters can be requested. The initial fee is $150 and a $50 per year use fee over and above the normal annual vehicle registration charges.

To trace the owner of a NWT registered vehicle the general public must contact the R.C.M.P in Yellowknife for this information.

YUKON

CFWH 570 Whitehorse
CKRW 610 Whitehorse

WHITEHORSE

AM RADIO

ABC12
1 PLATE VALIDATED BY
2 DECALS

LONDON
PERSONALIZED
2 PLATES ISSUED

1234
PASSENGER OLDER ISSUE
USED UNTIL JUNE 92

MPA123
ROYAL CDN
MTD POLICE

YTG901
YUKON TERRITORIAL
GOVERNMENT

FGA 21
FEDERAL GOVERNMENT

FGA 21
RENTAL VEHICLE

COA 46
LIGHT COMMERCIAL
VEHICLE

COA 45
HEAVY COMMERCIAL
VEHICLE

DLR 027
DEALER

Yukon Territory passenger plates have 3 alpha - 1 or 2 numeric characters. They have no codes. However the renewal month is assigned by the first initial of the owner's last name or the first letter of a corporate name. Other classes of vehicles can be identified by the alpha prefix on the plate:

C - Commercial
D,DLR - Dealer
F - Farm
FG - Federal Government
G, YTG - Yukon Government
M - Motorcycle, moped
R - Rented vehicle
S - Snowmobile
T - Trailer
VY1 - Ham radio call letters

First letter of name or corporation	Renewal Month
F or H	January
M	February
B	March
D,V,O or E	April
N or T	May
W, Y, or R	July
K,J, or I	August
C, Q, or X	September
A or P	October
S,U, or Z	November
G or L	December

Personalized plates are available from Motor Vehicle Dept. Box 2703 Whitehorse Y1A 2C6. Fee $100 tax included, plus normal registration fee. 6 characters allowed.
To trace a vehicle, contacted Whitehorse DMV. Reason must be approved Fee $6

PLATE FACTS

In the space age, we still have ties to the horse and buggy days. Horseless Carriage license plates are issued to collectors of vintage vehicles, while Hawaii still issues a plate for a horse drawn wagon. Alabama trucks restricted to a 15 mile operating area are issued plates called "mule tags" valid for the same area a mule can travel in one day.

Personalized or "vanity" plates are a further extension of the love affair with the automobile. Motorists in Minnesota pay an extra $100 just for the privilege of having their name, initials or favorite saying on their license plates. However the thrifty New Englanders in Maine pay only $15 extra for the same indulgence. All states now offer their motorists the opportunity to personalize their plates and plate"spotting" has become more intriguing. Most states refer to these special plates as" personalized" or "vanity" plates, however a number of states have different names for them . Both Wyoming and New Mexico call them "Prestige", while Oregon refers to them as "Custom". In Canada the term is "PNP" for personalized number plates. California, which has issued well over one million personalized plates calls them "Environmental" License Plates" or simply "ELP's" as the revenue generated goes to environmental projects. In pursuit of additional revenue, several states have begun promoting these plates very actively. Both New York and North Carolina have expanded their manufacturing die capability to accommodate up to 8 characters.

Computers and efficiency experts are gradually making county and geographical codes on license plates obsolete. In 1964, twenty five states had either a county, congressional district or police troop code on their passenger car plates. In 1991 only 10 states continue this practice. Many states have decided to use county name decals on license plates. States are encouraged to standardize their numbering system to 3 alpha- 3 numeric which can accommodate 17 million combinations without duplications. As a result of modern radio and computer technology, law enforcement officers do not have to rely as heavily on county codes for quick vehicle identification. Ten states are currently issuing plates where the county is identified by name sticker or embossing.

State slogans, mottos and commercials for local industry have traditionally appeared on license plates. Arizona calls your attention to its Grand Canyon, Idaho promotes its famous potatoes, Maine its Vacationland, and the indian "zia" sun symbol adds to the enchantment of New Mexico.

Plates provide an opportunity to honor individuals who have served their country. Many states now issue special plates to recipients of the Congressional Medal of Honor, Purple Heart and survivors of the attack on Pearl Harbor. War veterans are and retired military personnel can obtain special plates. Each state list of special plates is different, and the lists are increasing every year.

SPECIAL PLATES

The latest plate craze sweeping the nation is the increased availability of special category license plates. These range from: Veteran plates (recognizing past military service and major decorations) to a myriad of college and university tags (now available in two dozen states) to the Baltimore Professional Duckpin Bowling Association special plate issued in Maryland.

Florida, with good reason, now views license plates as an important source of revenue. They have successfully raised vast amounts of money for specific causes through the use of special plates. These include The Astronauts Memorial which is funded by the Challenger plate. The endangered Florida manatee and panther each have their own fund-raising plates (the manatee plate is more popular than the panther). The 25th Anniversary of the Super Bowl, 500th Anniversary of Christopher Columbus discovering America and now the 20th anniversary of Disney World are recent and future projects.

One might wonder what the makers of the first license plates, 90 years ago, would think if they could see our plates today - - - - Mickey Mouse on a license plate? When one really thinks about it - - why not ? License plates are not that different from postage stamps - enjoy them, save and collect them, and some day they might become very valuable.

COLLECTING LICENSE PLATES

Most states and provinces have sample plates available, and this is a good way to start a collection. The cost varies from as high as $10 for the popular Northwest Territories bear plate to some jurisdictions who will send one at no charge. The prices and policies vary from state to state. Write to each DMV. You can use the address in this book. Georgia is the only state that does not offer samples.

A typical American family garage will have old license plates hanging on the wall. Most recent plates are recycled, but not too many years ago new plates were issued yearly and the old ones discarded. Most of us at some time have wondered if these souvenirs have anything but sentimental value. The answer is probably no, except to a collector hobbyist, and even then, it depends on the condition of the plate and its rarity.

If you would like to know more about the plates you own, or even become a collector, contact the Automobile License Plate Collectors Association. This is a non profit national organization of license plate collectors, hobbyists and enthusiasts. ALPCA publishes a bimonthly newsletter with articles about old license plates and advertisements to buy, sell or trade among its members. For further information contact:

Gary Brent Kincade, Secretary
Automobile License Plate Collectors Association
P.O. Box 77
Horner, West Virginia, 26372

TEST YOUR LICENSE PLATE KNOWLEDGE

Here is a quiz about U.S. passenger license plates. Its for all ages, but some of the questions are tough! The answers are at the bottom of the page.

1. How many of the 20 states that require only one plate can you name?

2 . You need to identify only 6 states to find a total of 8 animals -(2 horses, 1 colt, 2 pelicans,1 lobster, 1 mountain goat and a song bird).

3. Saskatchewan has wheat on their plate, what 4 states promote their agricultural products on license plates?

4. People are important, and important people are on license plates. Can you name the 4 states that have plates that display either the image or name of a president?

5. Which state requires the registration of all vehicles every year, even those that are inoperable, in storage or otherwise not being driven?

6. When you look on a map, states have distinctive shapes. Can you name those ten states who use these outlines on their license plate ? Its tougher than you think!

7. Unless you are an expert, you will probably have to guess which state issues a Weed and Pest Control plate. A hint - the first number on this state's passenger plate is a county code.

8. Do you know which state is the last to use reflective sheeting for a general issue of license plates? Probably not , but we have to put one question in for the experts. But to give you a hint, it is the same state where an elected county official's plate could be captioned "FREEHOLDER".

9. When you are big you like to wave the flag. Can you name two states who proudly display a flag on their plates?

10. Which state, territory or province issues the most beautiful license plate? This should start a discussion, and believe it or not, there is an answer!

1. AL, AZ, AR, DE, FL, GA, IN, KS, KY, LA, MA, MI, MS, NM, NC, OK, PA, SC, TN, WV.
2. KY (1 horse, 1 colt). LA (2 pelicans), ME (1 lobster), NV (1 mountain goat), SC (1 bird), WY (1 horse bucking) 3 GA (peach), ID (famous potatoes), KS (wheat),NJ (Garden State) .
4. IL (Land of Lincoln), SD (Mt Rushmore),VA (Washington is on the Centennial plate), WA (State name). 5. A new California law 6. CT, FL, IN, MN, MT, NJ, OH, OK, TX, WV.)
7. Wyoming . 8. NJ 9. AK, TX.. 10. Members of ALPCA (Automobile License Plate Collector's Assn.) every year selects the most beautiful North American license plate . The winning jurisdiction receives an award. (Recent winners have been South Carolina, Oklahoma and Nova Scotia).

LICENSE PLATE GAMES

Motorists have discovered license plate spotting games are a great activity to help pass long hours on the highway. Make up your own rules, everyone can play, and all you need is a good pair of eyes, and maybe a pad and pencil. And as a word of advice, make it clear in the beginning that the driver is the final judge in all disputes - - exactly like the captain of a ship at sea!

Easy games:

Identify colors on a plate, find letters of the alphabet and numbers in sequence. Pick a "magic" two digit number or initials to see on a plate. Another variation is to pick a color and only the plates on that color vehicle "count".

Competitive games(fun for all ages):

SPELL THE SHORTEST WORD - Use the letters on a plate in the sequence they appear, and by adding letters construct the shortest word possible. Example : MLN-123 makes **MainLinE** (8 letters) while **MeLoN** wins with 5 letters.

POKER- The first three numbers on the first plate you see is the start of your hand. Using the first two numbers on the next plate you have a basic poker hand. Make your wager, declare your discards (up to 3 numbers) and watch the next plate to draw your final hand. A variation is to use truck five digit plates.

DICE - Use the first number or numbers on a plate to determine dice combinations. If the first digits are 2 - 9, 11,12 use as is. If it is 13 - 19 add them together. For example13 becomes 4 (1+3). The first plate you see is your "roll". If the roll is 7 or 11 you win; 2 or 3 you lose; 12 you lose but keep your turn going first. All other possible sums (4,5,6,8,9,10) is your "point". To win, you must see your "Point" as the first numbers on a plate before one that begins with 7 or 16 which is the same as 7.

BLAZE A TRAIL - The object of this game is to "Blaze a trail" from coast to coast or between any two points of your choice- perhaps between New Jersey and Arizona if that is the destination of the trip. Look for license plates from states that border each other until you have a trail that connects your two points. Players take turns with time limits, or have only certain color vehicles to choose from. One rule is you must see a plate of a state that borders one you have seen to continue your "trail". You cannot see a plate out of sequence and "save" it for future use.

One last thought- make the person spotting a plate name the capital of the state or province before they can claim it in any game.